Winning the Study Game

Learning How to Succeed in School

Consumable Student Edition

Lawrence J. Greene

Peytral Publications, Inc.
Minnetonka, MN 55345
952-949-8707

Winning the Study Game: Learning How to Succeed in School
Consumable Student Edition by Lawrence J. Greene

© 2002 by Lawrence J. Greene
10 9 8 7 6 5 4 3 2
Printed and bound in the United States of America

All rights reserved. The consumable student edition is for individual student use only. No part of the book may be reproduced, stored in a retrieval system, or transmitted in any form or by any means, electronic, mechanical, photocopying or otherwise, without prior written permission from the copyright owner.

All names or people and places used in this book are fictional. Any similarity to actual individuals or situations is coincidental.

Publisher's Cataloging-in-Publication
(Provided by Quality Books, Inc.)

Greene, Lawrence J.
Winning the study game : learning how to succeed in school / Lawrence J. Greene. -- Consumable student ed.
p. cm.
ISBN: 1-890455-47-4

1. Learning disabled teenagers--Education (Secondary)
2. Study skills--Handbooks, manuals, etc. 3. Special education--Handbooks, manuals, etc. I. Title.

LC4704.74.G74 2002 371.9'0430281
QBI02-200428

Library of Congress Control Number: 2002107590
ISBN: 1-890455-47-4

Published by: *Peytral Publications, Inc.*
PO Box 1162
Minnetonka, MN 55345
(952) 949-8707
www.peytral.com

Table of Contents

Introduction

Did you ever think about why some kids in your class get good grades? Well, the reasons are simple. They know how to study for tests. They're organized. They plan ahead. They can remember important information.

If you're not doing as well as you would like in school, you ***can*** turn things around. Just as you can be taught to become a better basketball player, you can also be taught how to become a better student. If you were on the basketball team, your coach would put you through drills every day during practice. These drills would not only build your strength and stamina, they would also teach you the fundamentals of the game. You would practice until passing the ball or making a lay-up becomes second nature.

To become a top-notch *academic athlete,* you also need to practice until you learn the fundamentals. You must acquire good study habits, and you must practice using these skills until you learn them and make them a habit.

If you apply the methods you are going to learn in this book every day in school, you can be certain that your grades will improve. Your teacher or resource specialist will be your "coach" and will guide you through the program. As you use the methods, you'll discover that your academic and thinking skills are improving day by day. Before long, you'll be amazed by how well you can study and learn.

Enough said. It's time to learn how to be a winner in school. Let's get started.

Important Note: Write your name on the cover of this workbook and insert it in your binder after you do work in it. You will want to keep the book for review and reference, not only this year but in the years ahead. It will be your guide through high school. The tools you learn will make your life easier! Don't lose the book! If you do, you'll regret it.

Part 1

Getting Organized

Unit 1

Developing a Personal Study Plan

The Daily Homework Battle

It had been a difficult day. Joshua's teacher had gotten angry at him for not paying attention during the science lesson, and, as usual, he didn't do very well on the weekly vocabulary test or the math quiz. But now school was finally over, and he was free to do other things and have some fun.

As soon as he went through the front door, Joshua heaved his book bag into the corner and raced to the kitchen. On the way, he yelled hello to his mom and petted his yellow lab whose tail was beating back and forth. Opening the refrigerator, Joshua grabbed the milk carton. He slammed the door shut, reached in the cabinet for a glass, and filled it with milk. He then picked up the two chocolate chip cookies his mother had left for him on a plate near the stove. Ten gulps later, he was ready to head outside. As he dashed out the back door, he grabbed his basketball. Positioning himself ten feet from the hoop his dad had mounted above the garage door, Joshua began taking jump shots. Two minutes later, his friend Zachary showed up, and the game began. Joshua and Zachary went one-on-one.

Joshua was shooting well, and many of his shots went through the basket without even hitting the rim. He could sense that he was on his way to victory. The frustration he saw in Zachary's face told him that his friend also realized that Joshua was going to win the first game.

In the back of his mind, Joshua was aware of what was going to happen in a few minutes. His mother would soon call him to come inside and start his homework even though he had only

1 ~~How~~ what methods are used for Improving Farming?
2 What computers are being used in Medical Research?
3 What are Killer Bees?
4 How can ~~you~~ Illegal Drugs be controlled?
5 Why was Winning the War of Independence Important?

~~6~~
6 War -- ~~A~~ America vs. Japan
7 Branches Of the United States
8 Protecting Crops from Hungry Insects
9 Shark ~~Att~~ Attacks
10 Studying Weather Patterns
11 Studing ~~Ev~~ Effectively

12 How do you Distinguishing Ordinary Light from Laser Light?

13 How are Lasers used?

been playing basketball for less than a half hour. It happened the same way every day. Their battle had become a daily ritual. He would get home from school, have milk and cookies, and go outside to shoot baskets. Then his mother would ruin everything! She always insisted that he start his homework before dinner. They would then get into a big argument. His mother would become angry and threaten to tell his father that he wouldn't do his homework. After a great deal of yelling, Joshua would finally go up to his room, open his book bag, and begin working. He had no choice but to give in, but he felt angry, frustrated, and picked on.

Joshua hated doing homework. Being required to do more work after spending seven painful hours in school seemed like a cruel punishment. Just getting his mind to focus on reading took his total effort and concentration. Sounding out the difficult words and making sense out of the information was exhausting. Joshua knew it would take him forever to write the answers to the assigned questions at the end of the history unit, and he knew doing the fifteen math problems would take at least a half hour. It didn't make any difference anyway. He was certain that his teacher would return his assignments with red marks all over them.

"Why do the work if it's going to be wrong anyway?" he asked himself with frustration.

Joshua felt the time before dinner belonged to him. He would tell his parents that he could finish his assignments after he ate. The problem was that he always wanted to watch television after dinner, and his mom and dad knew it. When he turned on the television, there would be another argument.

"Why are they always bugging me?" Joshua thought angrily.

Because he hardly ever wrote down his assignments, Joshua was never really sure what was due the next day. To get his parents "off his back," he would either tell them that the teacher hadn't assigned any homework or that he had done his homework in school. This strategy seldom worked. His parents didn't believe him. They would remind him what his English teacher had said during their last conference: "I always assign homework." Then Joshua's parents would bring out his last report card and show him the teacher's comments. She wrote that Joshua often didn't hand in his assignments and that the work he did hand in was usually incomplete. Whenever they brought this up, Joshua knew he had lost the argument. Frustrated and resentful, he would turn off the TV and go to his room and begin his homework. He would give in, but he still felt mad. It was all so unfair.

Predicting What Will Happen

Do you think that the daily struggle between Joshua and his parents about homework is very predictable? When events happen over and over and take place in a certain expected order, these events can be described as a ritual.

> **Ritual:** something that occurs over and over in the same way.

Do you have any rituals in your own life? If so, list a few of your rituals below. (Hint: one might be drinking milk and eating a cookie every afternoon when you get home from school.)

My Rituals

1. ________________________________
2. ________________________________
3. ________________________________
4. ________________________________

Go back into the story and underline one time each event described in paragraph two that would happen after Joshua returned from school. (Hint: "Joshua heaved his book bag into the corner.") Then number each underlined event in the order in which it happened.

Now go back and circle each of Joshua's behaviors and attitudes that describe **how he feels about school and homework**. (Hint: "Joshua hated doing his homework.") Then number each attitude and behavior in the order in which it happened.

Write down each of the circled and numbered **behaviors and attitudes.** See if you can find at least six in the story. Once you write down the behaviors and attitudes, evaluate them in terms of how smart they are.

1: ________________________________

How would you evaluate this behavior or attitude?

1 2 3 4 5 6 7 8 9 10

Not Smart **Fairly Smart** **Very Smart**

Briefly tell why you evaluated the behavior or attitude in this way: ________________

____

____

2: ______________________________

How would you evaluate this behavior or attitude?

1 2 3 4 5 6 7 8 9 10

Not Smart **Fairly Smart** **Very Smart**

Briefly tell why you evaluated the behavior or attitude in this way: ______________________________

____

____

3: ______________________________

How would you evaluate this behavior or attitude?

1 2 3 4 5 6 7 8 9 10

Not Smart **Fairly Smart** **Very Smart**

Briefly tell why you evaluated the behavior or attitude in this way: ______________________________

____

____

4: ______________________________

How would you evaluate this behavior or attitude?

1 2 3 4 5 6 7 8 9 10

Not Smart **Fairly Smart** **Very Smart**

Briefly tell why you evaluated the behavior or attitude in this way: ______________________________

____

____

5: ______________________________

How would you evaluate this behavior or attitude?

1 2 3 4 5 6 7 8 9 10

Not Smart **Fairly Smart** **Very Smart**

Briefly tell why you evaluated the behavior or attitude in this way: ______________________________

____

____

6: hardly ever write down his assignments

How would you evaluate this behavior or attitude?

1 **2** **3** **4** **5** **6** **7** **8** **9** **10**

Not Smart **Fairly Smart** **Very Smart**

Briefly tell why you evaluated the behavior or attitude in this way:

he might forget

Make three predictions about the consequences of Joshua's behaviors and attitudes. The consequences could happen in school or at home. (Example "He would get poor grades on his homework assignments.") Write the consequences below and circle whether you believe your predictions are **possible** (could occur) or **probable** (very likely to occur).

1. he will get bad grades

Possible **Probable**

2. he will have [illegible]

Possible **Probable**

3. he will get in trouble with his parents

Possible **Probable**

Let's pretend that Joshua decides that he really wants to do better in school. What changes in his attitude and behavior might help him to be more successful in school?

1. he will pay attention more
2. he will do his homework everyday
3. he will study more
4. he will turn in his homework
5. he will write down his assignments

Evaluate Joshua's overall plan for doing his homework.

1 **2** **3** **4** **5** **6** **7** **8** **9** **10**

Ineffective **Fairly Effective** **Very Effective**

Thinking and Planning Ahead

Let's say that Joshua is your friend, and he tells you that he wants to do better in school. He asks if you have any ideas that could help him. You suggest that he create a study schedule that would also leave enough time for him to do fun things.

Joshua's first step in developing a study schedule would be to list all of his subjects and estimate how much time he needs to spend every day doing his homework in each subject. You may be thinking, *"How can I make an estimate if I don't know what Joshua's homework assignments are and if I don't know how long it takes him to complete his reading assignment or do his math problems?"* This is true. You cannot tell the exact amount of time that he needs to spend doing homework without knowing his assignments and without knowing how good his skills are. However, based upon how much homework you do, you can probably estimate how much time Joshua generally needs to spend each evening. You would have to assume that he has similar academic skills and that it would take him approximately the same time to complete an assignment as it would take you.

Joshua's teacher, of course, may assign more homework, or less homework than your teacher. Your estimate, however, is likely to be fairly accurate.

Write your estimates below. Use minutes instead of hours (for example: Math -- 15 minutes.) You can change the actual subjects if you are taking different courses.

Joshua's Subjects

Approximate Amount of Daily Study Time Required

English	________
Math	________
Social Studies	________
Science	________
Government	________

As you know, some evenings you need to spend less time doing homework in a particular subject, and some evenings you need to spend more. For example, if you have a math test on Friday, you would need to spend more time studying Thursday evening.

By using your own study requirements as a guide, you could make your estimates even more realistic. You could figure out the *average time* he should study every evening in each of his subjects. This means taking the total time he needs to study every week in each subject and dividing this total by four (Monday, Tuesday, Wednesday, and Thursday).

Don't concern yourself now with how much homework and studying Joshua should do over the weekend. Some teachers assign homework over the weekend, and some do not. If you do have weekend homework assigned, you can make up a weekend schedule for Friday through Sunday.

Let's look at English. Let's say that for Joshua to do well on the English vocabulary quiz that is given every Friday, you believe that he needs to study his assigned vocabulary words for a total of 60 minutes each week. You also think that he needs to spend extra time reviewing on Wednesday and Thursday evening so that he's prepared for the test. Let's see how you could figure out his *average daily study time.*

Your Estimate of Weekly Time Required to Study Vocabulary Words

Monday	10 minutes
Tuesday	10 minutes
Wednesday	15 minutes
Thursday	25 minutes for final review
Total Weekly Study Time	**60 minutes**
Average Time Each Night	***15 minutes*** (60 minutes divided by 4 nights)

You would now plug 15 minutes after the subject English written on the above chart. Of course, there are other English assignments he would need to do such as book reports. You would have to factor extra time into Joshua's estimated time for these additional assignments. You might decide that on average he would have to spend an additional fifteen minutes each evening. Some evenings he might only have to study vocabulary and do some grammar exercises. Other evenings he would have to spend extra time writing an essay, reading his textbook and answering questions, or reading a book for a book report. You might estimate that Joshua should spend a total of 30 minutes each evening on English. You would follow the same time-averaging procedure for estimating Joshua's required study time in the other subjects listed on the chart.

Let's assume that Joshua agrees with your estimate and agrees to spend thirty minutes on average doing his English homework. Let's also assume that he works hard and concentrates when he studies. Predict the possible consequences.

Do you think Joshua's overall performance in English will improve? **Yes No Not Sure**

Do you think Joshua's performance on the weekly quiz will improve? **Yes No Not Sure**

How will Joshua feel if he begins to do well on the vocabulary quizzes?

1 2 3 4 5 6 7 8 9 10

No Different Somewhat Better Much Better

How will Joshua's parents feel if he begins to do well on the vocabulary quizzes?

1 2 3 4 5 6 7 8 9 10

No Different Somewhat Better Much Better

How will Joshua's teacher feel if he begins to do well on the vocabulary quizzes?

1 2 3 4 5 6 7 8 9 10

No Different Somewhat Better Much Better

How will Joshua's resource specialist feel if he begins to do well on the vocabulary quizzes?

1 2 3 4 5 6 7 8 9 10

No Different Somewhat Better Much Better

How motivated will Joshua be to continue using his schedule if he begins to do well on the quizzes?

1 2 3 4 5 6 7 8 9 10

Not Motivated Somewhat Motivated Very Motivated

Evaluate the overall effectiveness of the of the new study schedule:

1 2 3 4 5 6 7 8 9 10

Not Effective Fairly Effective Very Effective

Of course, you also realize that the *quality* of Joshua's studying will affect the outcome. If he develops an effective system for learning the words, concentrates, and works diligently (hard), this will certainly improve his performance on the weekly vocabulary quiz.

Making Your Own Study Schedule

It's now time for you to make your own study schedule. Before you begin, look at the sample schedule on the next page. Let's assume that this is the schedule Joshua created after estimating his average study time for each subject. You can see that the schedule indicates the time between when Joshua gets home from school each day until bedtime. The hours have been divided into ½- hour blocks of time. At the bottom of the schedule, you will find a code. As this book is not printed in color, picture patterns are used to indicate the ways Joshua has decided to use his time after school. For example, one geometric pattern represents the time he spends eating. Another represents free time. And another represents study time.

Note that this schedule allows Joshua to spend time with his friends for an hour before he begins his homework. Obviously, this arrangement will have to be worked out with his mom. It's likely, however, that she would agree to allow Joshua free time for an hour before starting his homework if she was convinced that he would:

1. keep to his agreements and maintain the schedule
2. study for an hour before dinner
3. study for an hour after dinner
4. have enough time to complete his assignments

Also note that Joshua's study schedule is based on spending a total of two and ½- hour doing homework every school night. Some students will require more study time, and some wil require less. Of course, even if two and ½- hours is usually sufficient for Joshua to complete hi homework, there may be situations in which additional homework will be required.

For example, he may have a book report due on Friday, and he may have to spend extra tim proofreading his report and checking for spelling and grammar errors. The same thing would be tru if he has a big exam on Wednesday. He may need extra time to review and study his notes.

There is also another possibility. His teacher may actually assign less homework on a particular night. Joshua's parents may allow him to do less homework that night, or they may wan him to use the two hours to organize his binder or get a head start on the next day's assignments.

Joshua might also decide to use the study time he scheduled to read a book for his next book report. This would certainly reduce the pressure to him to complete the book and his book report on time.

Joshua's Weekly Schedule

TIME:	Monday	Tuesday	Wednesday	Thursday	Friday
3:15 - 3:30	xxxxxxxxx	xxxxxxxxxx	xxxxxxxxxxxxx	xxxxxxxxxxxx	
3:30 - 4:00	xxxxxxxxx	xxxxxxxxxx	xxxxxxxxxxxxx	xxxxxxxxxxxx	
4:00 - 4:30	xxxxxxxxx	xxxxxxxxxx	xxxxxxxxxxxxx	xxxxxxxxxxxx	
4:30 - 5:00	*********	*********	************	************	
5:00 - 5:30	*********	*********	************	************	
5:30 - 6:00	*********	*********	************	************	
6:00 - 6:30	^^^^^^^^^^^	^^^^^^^^^^^^	^^^^^^^^^^^^^^^	^^^^^^^^^^^^^^^	
6:30 - 7:00	xxxxxxxxx	xxxxxxxxx	xxxxxxxxxxxxx	xxxxxxxxxxxxx	
7:00 - 7:30	*********	*********	************	************	
7:30 - 8:00	*********	*********	************	************	
8:00 - 8:30	xxxxxxxxx	xxxxxxxxx	xxxxxxxxxxxxx	xxxxxxxxxxxxx	
8:30 - 9:00	xxxxxxxxx	xxxxxxxxx	xxxxxxxxxxxxx	xxxxxxxxxxxxx	
9:00 - 9:30	xxxxxxxxx	xxxxxxxxx	xxxxxxxxxxxxx	xxxxxxxxxxxxx	
9:30 -10:00	zzzzzzzzzzz	zzzzzzzzzzz	zzzzzzzzzzzzzz	zzzzzzzzzzzzzz	

Code: [x] free time [*] studying [^] dinner [z] sleep

Deciding how much time you need to spend studying and creating a personal study schedule can actually be fun. There is another major advantage. If you create a schedule and use it, you will be amazed by how much free time you will have to play, watch TV, talk on the phone with your friends, use your computer, or do other things you enjoy.

It's now time for you to create your own study schedule.

Steps For Making Your Own Study Schedule

Step 1: Write down the subjects you are taking and then write in the average number of minutes you need to spend each week in each subject. Then divide by 4 (Monday – Thursday) to determine the average study time you need to spend **every day** in each subject.

My Subjects	Approximate Amount of Daily Study Time Required
____________	______
____________	______
____________	______
____________	______
____________	______
____________	______
Total Daily Study Time:	______

Step 2: Write down the times you get home from school, have dinner, and go to bed.

Get home from school: ____________

Dinner time: ____________

Bed time: ____________

These times usually do not change. Unless your parents decide you can stay up later or change the dinner time, you can probably count on dinner and bedtime being at a certain time during the week. There may be occasional exceptions, but this will probably not happen very often.

Now you are ready to use the information to complete your own schedule. Look at the schedule on page 16. It indicates the time between getting home from school each day and going to bed. Before you attempt to complete the schedule, read the instructions carefully. Plan what you want to do before you begin to fill in the schedule. Ask your teacher if she can give you a practice schedule before you actually color the schedule in your workbook. By filling out the practice schedule first, you can make changes. Once you are satisfied with your schedule, you can complete the one in your book. Later you can adjust the schedule as your school obligations change or when you enter the next grade. (As you progress through school, you are likely to find that you have more homework and that more study time is required.)

Step 3: Use different-colored pencils or felt pens to indicate when you eat dinner and when you go to bed. If you prefer, you can be creative and use geometric designs to indicate the different activities. Let's say that you eat between 6:00 and 6:45. Fill in that time every day in a color or design of your choice. For example, you might choose red for eating. If you eat between 6:00 and 6:45 color in one and one half strips. Below the schedule, fill in one of the little boxes with the selected color or design and write "Dinner Time." Fill in the second box with another color and write "Bed Time."

Step 4: Now use a different color or design to indicate when you want to study and do homework. For example, you might want to do homework from 5:00 to 6:00. Dinner might be from 6:00 to 6:45. You might want to have some time for yourself until 7:00 and then do your remaining homework until 8:00 or 8:30 PM. (Remember to fill in the code below to indicate what the colors or geometric designs mean.)

Step 5: Use a different color to indicate when you want to have free time, make telephone calls, or watch TV. For example, if you get home from school at 3:30 and want to play basketball or get together with friends until 5:00, color in the time on the schedule in the color you have chosen. Below the schedule, fill in the little box with the color or design you have selected and write "Free Time."

Step 6: Show your schedule to your teacher, resource specialist, and parents to see if they have any suggestions. If they do not, and you are happy with it, then you have created a study schedule that should make your life easier and more organized.

Step 7: As an experiment, keep using your schedule for at least two weeks. See if your grades improve and school becomes easier.

Step 8: Observe how your schedule is working. After a two-week trial period, you may want to fine-tune the schedule. This means making changes that will improve the schedule and make it even more effective. For example, you may find that you need to spend approximately ten additional minutes each evening doing your science assignment and ten less minutes doing your math assignment. Remember, your schedule should be your friend, and not your enemy!

My Weekly Schedule

TIME	Monday	Tuesday	Wednesday	Thursday	Friday
3:15 - 3:30					
3:30 - 4:00					
4:00 - 4:30					
4:30 - 5:00					
5:00 - 5:30					
5:30 - 6:00					
6:00 - 6:30					
6:30 - 7:00					
7:00 - 7:30					
7:30 - 8:00					
8:00 - 8:30					
8:30 - 9:00					
9:00 - 9:30					
9:30 -10 :00					

Code: [ ] free time [ ] studying [ ] dinner [ ] sleep [ ] ______________ *

[ ] ______________ [ ] ______________ [ ] ______________

*** religious school, music practice, Scouts, after-school athletics, tutoring, chores, etc.**

Step 9: Record your grades in every subject (tests, essays, reports, special projects, etc.) once you begin using your study schedule. Do this for the two-week trial period while you are fine-tuning your schedule. This will help you track your improvement and it will help you make adjustments. If, for example, your grade in math does not improve, you may need to schedule more time to do math homework and studying. (See page 68 for a grade-tracking form.)

The secret to making the schedule work is to keep to it, even if this means making some sacrifices. For example, you may want to watch a football game on TV, but the game may be on when you are supposed to be studying. Turning off the TV can be difficult, but keeping your commitments must be your top priority (i.e., your most important obligation). To get value from your schedule and experience the positive results, you have to maintain your schedule even when there are powerful temptations to abandon it. This means coming in and starting your homework when *you* agreed to begin without having to be reminded. It also means studying during the times *you* determined, even if there is something else you would rather be doing. When you feel like giving in to the temptation, you'll need to remind yourself that you made an agreement and that you keep your agreements.

Keeping to your schedule is similar to maintaining an athletic training program. If you want to be on the track team, you may decide to run three miles every morning during the summer vacation. Because you want to run before it gets too hot, you decide to get up early and run at 7:00 AM. Let’s say that one morning you want to sleep in and skip running that day. There’s a good chance that you may begin to find many other reasons not to run. Each time you skip your daily run, it will become easier and easier to justify giving up your commitment. Before long you may totally abandon your training regimen.

My Personal Study-Schedule Contract

The following "contract" will help you maintain your schedule. It will remind you of your commitment. Keeping commitments is an important part of thinking and acting smart.

My Study-Schedule Contract

To Whom It May Concern:

I, ______________________________ (your name), agree to use my study schedule every day for a **2-week trial period.** If I decide after two weeks that the schedule needs to be adjusted, I can make changes. Once I make these changes, I agree to use the new schedule for a minimum of **4 additional weeks**. If I am pleased with the results and my school work improves, I will continue to use the schedule for the rest of the school year. I can make changes in the schedule every four weeks. Once I make these adjustments, I will use the schedule for another four weeks before making changes.

Finally, I agree to keep to my schedule without having to be reminded by my parents.

Your Signature : ______________________ **Date:** ______________

Your Teacher's Signature: ______________________ **Your Parent's Signature:** ______________________

Study Breaks

Everyone needs to take an occasional break when studying. Taking a break, however, does not mean getting up every four minutes to walk around the house, talk with your brother, take a look at TV, or call a friend on the telephone.

Successful students train themselves to work for a set period of time before taking time out for a rest. This is called a training regimen. Successful athletes know the value of a consistent training regimen. A football player may go to the weight room three times a week and spend an hour there. A karate student may go to class three times a week and spend two hours practicing kicks. These athletes condition themselves to work until they complete the daily regimen. They may take some breaks, but no matter how tired they are, they don't stop until they finish. Over time, they build their endurance to the point that they don't get very tired.

General Formula for Taking Study Breaks

4th & 5th Grade:	study or do homework for a minimum of **fifteen to twenty minutes** before taking a **five-minute break**.
6th & 7th Grade:	study or do homework for a minimum of **twenty to twenty-five minutes** before taking a **five-minute break.**
8th & 9th Grade:	study or do homework for a minimum of **twenty-five minutes to thirty minutes** before taking a **five-minute break.**
10th & 11th Grade	study or do homework for a minimum of **twenty-five to thirty-five minutes** before taking a **five minute break.**

Some students who can concentrate for longer periods of time may prefer to study for 25 to 35 minutes before taking a rest. If you find at first that you cannot work for twenty minutes at a time, you should set up your own *personal training program* to build up your study stamina (strength and endurance). You might use an egg timer. The first day you start your training program, you could set the timer for 10 minutes. When the buzzer goes off, you can take a five-minute rest. The next day you would set the timer at 11 minutes. Each day you would add one minute to the time you study before taking your break. Before you know it, you will be able to study for twenty minutes at a time!

Taking too many breaks when studying can interfere with doing good work. Training your brain is just like training your body in sports. With practice, your skills will improve, and you will get stronger and develop more endurance. The scheduling procedures will become a habit, and you will become increasingly comfortable with using them.

What I Have Learned about Schedules

Circle T (True), F (False), S (Sometimes), or N/S (Not Sure)

Making a schedule is too "boring."	T	F	S	N/S
Making a schedule is "dumb."	T	F	S	N/S
You don't need to use your schedule consistently.	T	F	S	N/S
Schedules can make life easier.	T	F	S	N/S
Schedules will take away from my fun time.	T	F	S	N/S
Schedules should never be changed.	T	F	S	N/S
You can build "free time" into a schedule.	T	F	S	N/S
Schedules can't help me get better grades.	T	F	S	N/S
Schedules can help me get my homework done more quickly.	T	F	S	N/S
If you're doing OK in school, you don't need a schedule.	T	F	S	N/S
Having and keeping to a schedule can reduce parent "nagging."	T	F	S	N/S
Taking study breaks every 5 minutes helps you to study better.	T	F	S	N/S

Unit 2

Recording Your Assignments

Knowing What You're Supposed to Do and When It's Due

History class was almost over, thank goodness. The class could not end soon enough for Heather. As usual, she felt overwhelmed by the teacher's lecture, and she didn't want to participate in the class discussion. Heather was always afraid of saying something dumb and making a fool of herself. To avoid this, she would either drift off into her daydreams or focus on the pictures she was drawing in her binder.

Mr. Garvey began writing the homework assignment on the chalkboard. Thursday: history test, Chapter 3, Section 1 – "Know important dates of the War of Independence and conditions that led to war." After writing down the assignment, Mr. Garvey briefly discussed the test. He gave examples of the dates he wanted students to memorize, and he briefly reviewed some of the social conditions they had discussed in class that had caused the American colonies to revolt against England. Realizing that Mr. Garvey was giving important clues about what the test would cover, most of the students tried to write down everything that he was saying.

Maria transferred the information written on the board to her assignment organizer. She carefully recorded the date of the test. She also wrote down Mr. Garvey's clues. She knew these would help her prepare for the test.

While Mr. Garvey had his back to the class and was writing the assignment on the board, Heather was busy whispering to her best friend Sarah. She laughed at something Sarah told her, and she continued making designs on a piece of paper. On the top of the page of doodles, she scribbled "history test." She then began to read the note that Sarah had passed to her. It was about a cute new boy who had just moved into the house down the street from her.

Predicting What Will Happen

In Unit 1, you examined the way Joshua studied and the nightly battle he had with his mother about doing his homework. Based on his behavior and attitudes, you also made predictions about what was likely to happen.

Let's follow the same procedure here. Go back into the story. Using a pencil, underline each of Maria's behaviors, and number each behavior in the order in which it occurred. You should be able to find three. Then underline each of Heather's actions two times using a pen, and number them in the order which they occurred. You should be able to find three.

Write down each of Maria's behaviors that you underlined and numbered.

#1: wrote the information in her assignment organizer

How would you evaluate the behavior?

1 2 3 4 5 6 7 8 9 10

Not Smart **Fairly Smart** **Very Smart**

#2: recorded the date of the test

How would you evaluate the behavior?

1 2 3 4 5 6 7 8 9 10

Not Smart **Fairly Smart** **Very Smart**

#3: wrote down clues

How would you evaluate the behavior?

1 2 3 4 5 6 7 8 9 10

Not Smart **Fairly Smart** **Very Smart**

You can probably make some predictions about the consequences of Maria's behaviors. Under the consequence, circle whether you believe the outcome is possible or probable. *Possible* means it could happen. *Probable* means it is likely to happen

Her grades in school:

1 2 3 4 5 6 7 8 9 10 ***Possible*** ***Probable***

Poor **Average** **Excellent**

Her relationship with her parents:

1 2 3 4 5 6 7 8 9 10 *Possible* *Probable*

Poor Average Excellent

Her relationship with her teacher:

1 2 3 4 5 6 7 8 9 10 *Possible* *Probable*

Poor Average Excellent

Now do the same thing with each of Heather's behaviors. List them and evaluate them.

#1: Drawing in class

How would you evaluate the behavior?

1 2 3 4 5 6 7 8 9 10

Not Smart Fairly Smart Very Smart

#2: talking in class

How would you evaluate the behavior?

1 2 3 4 5 6 7 8 9 10

Not Smart Fairly Smart Very Smart

#3: daydreaming in class

How would you evaluate the behavior?

1 2 3 4 5 6 7 8 9 10

Not Smart Fairly Smart Very Smart

Now make some predictions about the consequences of Heather's behaviors.

Her grades in school:

1 2 3 4 5 6 7 8 9 10 *Possible* *Probable*

Poor Average Excellent

Her relationship with her parents:

1 2 3 4 5 6 7 8 9 10 *Possible* *Probable*

Poor Average Excellent

Her relationship with her teacher:

1	2	3	4	5	6	7	8	9	10		***Possible***	***Probable***
Poor				**Average**				**Excellent**				

Creating a Personal Homework-Recording System

Let's pretend that Heather is one of your friends. She tells you that her parents are upset about her grades, and they have said that they are going to ground her until her grades improve. Heather asks you if you have any ideas about how to improve her grades.

List four ideas that might help Heather do better in school.

1. whrite down her assighnments
2. Pay attention in class
3. write down usefull infromation
4. dont be distracted by other people

Perhaps your suggestions included:

- Ask the resource specialist for help
- Go to the teacher for extra help
- Spend more time studying
- Write down her assignments on an assignment sheet
- Check with a friend to make sure that she has her assignments accurately recorded
- Study with a friend who is getting good grades

Let's assume that you come up with four good suggestions, and Heather conscientiously follows your advice. Make some predictions about the consequences of her new behaviors.

Her grades in school:

1	2	3	4	5	6	7	8	9	10		***Possible***	***Probable***
Poor				**Average**				**Excellent**				

Her relationship with her parents:

1	2	3	4	5	6	7	8	9	10		***Possible***	***Probable***
Poor				**Average**				**Excellent**				

Her relationship with her teacher:

1	2	3	4	5	6	7	8	9	10	Possible	Probable
Poor				Average				Excellent			

Practice Writing Down Assignments

Look at the following homework assignment. Let's assume that your teachers have written these assignments on the chalkboard. Let's also assume that today is Monday.

Social Studies:	Due. Tues.
	Read pgs. 65-70
	Answer questions 1-8 pg. 71
	Complete sentences. Skip line between answers.
	Test on Chapter 2 Friday
Science:	Due. Wed.
	Read pgs. 82-91
	Know definitions of six words on pg. 71
Math:	Due Tues.
	pg. 49 problems 1-12
	pg. 51 problems 1-6
	show your work (not just the answers)
English:	Due Tues.
	Learn vocabulary words pgs. 71-77

As you can see, certain assignments are due on Tuesday. Other assignments are due later in the week. For example, the social studies teacher has scheduled a chapter test on Friday, and the science homework assignment is due Wednesday.

Not all teachers write assignments on the chalkboard. Some hand out a weekly assignment sheet. Others announce what the homework is at the end of class. Hearing assignments without seeing them written on the chalkboard or on a weekly assignment sheet can be difficult because you have to listen carefully while writing the key information in your assignment book.

Look at the **"Sample Assignment Sheet."** Typical homework assignments have been recorded on it. ***See page 28 for an explanation of the abbreviations that are used on the sheet.***

Sample Assignment Sheet

SUBJECTS	MONDAY	TUESDAY	WEDNESDAY	THURSDAY	FRIDAY
Math	*p. 117 – 118 prob. 1-12 s.w. l. – form – p 119*	*rvw. p.120-122 prob. 1-10 p.123 s.w. prob 1-5 p. 124 s.w.*	*l. form. p.126 p.127-130 s.w. Prob 1-12 p.130*	*p.131-135 prob. 1-10 p.136*	*rvw. for M.T.*
Social Studies	*ch. 4 rd, p. 82-90 Ans. ques. p.91 1-6 comp.sen.*	*Begin research for term paper ch-4 rd. p.91-98 Ans. ques. p.99 1-8 comp. sen.*	*Ch. 4 Take Notes*	*Ch.5 rd.p.102-110 Ans. ques. p.111 1-8*	*Ch. 5 rd.p.111-119 Ans. ques. p.118 1-8*
English	*Rd. poems p. 61-64 st. vocab words p.60*	*Write 10 sen. using voc. words p.65 prfrd. b.r.*	*Rd. p.66-72 Ans. ques. p. 73 1-7*	*Begin essay on poem p.76*	*Feb essay rd. book For b.r.*
Science	*U. 6 rd. p. 74 – 80 l. form p.81*	*rd. 82-90 Ans. ques. 1-8 p.91*	*Take notes p.81-90 rd. p. 92-99 Ans. ques. 1-6 p.100*	*l. form p.97 rd. 101-109 Ans. ques. 1-6 p.110*	*Study for U. 6 Science T.*
Tests & Reports	*Voc. Q. 2/25 Fri.*	*Math Q. 2/22 – Tues.*	*B.R. due 3/2 – Fri.*	*Sc. T. 3/2 U 6 – Fri. ch.4*	

It's time to practice using the assignment sheet. Transfer the assignments on page 25 to the **"Practice Assignment Sheet."** Use the **"Sample Assignment Sheet"** as a guide. To make the information fits, use abbreviations such as "Tues." for Tuesday and "pg." for page. (See page 28).

Practice Assignment Sheet

SUBJECTS	MONDAY	TUESDAY	WEDNESDAY	THURSDAY	FRIDAY
Math	D. Tues. pg 17 probs 1-8 (s.w)	D. wed. pg. 20 prob. 1-20 (s.w)	D. Thurs. pg. 25 prob 1-12 (s.w)	D. Fri. pg. 29 probs. 1-7 (s.w)	
Social Studies	D. Tues. Read pgs. 36-39	D. wed. Rd. pgs. 40-44 Chptr. 2. on Fri.	Rev w Thurs. for Fri. Quiz D. Thurs. pgs. 62-65 Exer. p. 66 1-6	Due Fri. pgs. 67-69 Exer p. 70 1-6	
English	D Tues. Adv. pgs. 81-83 Exer. p... 84 1-12	D. wed Rd. poems pgs. 87-89 Ques. 1-6 p. 91	D. Thurs. wrkbk pgs. 94-96	D. Fri. wrkbk pgs. 97-99 Exer. p. 99 1-8	
Science	D. Tues. pgs. 54-59 Exer. p. 60/ 1-8 Prac. Test wed.	D. wed Rd. pgs 61-66 Exer. p. 67/ 1-5	D Thurs. pgs. 67-73 Exer p. 76/1-6	Due Fri. Test	
Tests & Reports					

When using abbreviations, you must be able to understand what you have written. The following abbreviations will not only save space when you write information on your assignment sheet, they will also save time. Once you learn the abbreviations, you will be able to use them automatically. Just make certain that you can read what you write.

Mastery: More Practice Writing Down Assignments

Imagine that your teachers have written the following weekly homework assignments on the chalkboard. Transfer the information on page 29 to the *Practice Assignment Sheet II* on page 30.

Use the *Sample Assignment Sheet* as a guide when recording this information on the *Practice Assignment Sheet*. Write neatly. To make things fit, remember to use abbreviations whenever possible.

Common Abbreviations:

ans. = answer
b.r. = book report
ch. = chapter
comp. = complete
crct. = correct
d. = due
E. = exam
ex. = example
exer. = exercises
fin. = finish
F. = final exam
form.= formulas
hmw. = homework
l. = learn
M.T. = midterm
p. = page
prac. = practice
prob. = problems
prfrd. = proofread
Q. = quiz
ques. = question
rd. = read
rpt = report
rvw. = review
r.w. = rewrite
sen. = sentence
sp. = spell
st. = study
s.w. = show work
T. = test
U. = unit
wrkbk. = workbook

Assignments

Math:

D. Tues.
P. 17
probs 1-8 (s.w.)
D. Wed.
pg. 20 probs.1-12 (s.w.)
D. Thurs.
p. 25
prob. 1-12 (s.w))
D. Fri.
p. 29
probs. 1-7 (s.w.)

English:

D. Tues.
Adverbs pgs. 81-83
Exer. p.. 84 1-12
D. Wed.
Read poems p..87-89
Ques. 1-6 p 91
D. Thurs.
Wrkbk pgs. 94-96
Exer. p. 97 1-8
D. Fri.
Wrkbk pgs. 97-99
Exer p. 99 1-8

Science:

D. Tues.
pgs. 54-59
Exer. pg. 60 1-8
Prac. test Wed.
D. Wed.
Rd. pgs. 61-66
Exer. pg. 67 1-5
D. Thurs.
Pgs. 67-73
Exer. p. 76 1-6
Due Fri.
Test

Social Studies:

D. Tues.
Read pgs 36-39
D. Wed
Rd. pgs 40-44
Chap.2 on Fri.
Thurs. Revw Fri. Quiz
Due Thurs.
pgs. 62-65
Exer. p. 66 1-6
Due Fri.
pgs. 67-69
Exer. p. 70 1-6

Assignment Practice Sheet II

SUBJECTS	MONDAY	TUESDAY	WEDNESDAY	THURSDAY	FRIDAY
Math	NH	Pg. 17 P. 1-8 (S.W) D.	Pg. 20 P. 1-12 (S.W) D.	Pg. 25 D. P. 1-2 (S.W)	Pg. 29 1-7 (S.W) D
Social Studies	NH	read Pg. 36-39 D.	rd. pg. 40-44 D.	Pg. 62-65 exer. Pg. 66 1-6 D.	Pg. 67-69 exer. Pg. 70 1-6 D.
English	NH	adverbs. Pg. 81-83 exer. Pg. 84 1-12 D.	read poems Pg. 87-89 Q. 1-6 Pg. 91 D.	wrkbk. Pg. 90-94. exer. Pg. 97-99 D.	wrkbk. Pg. 94-96 exer. Pg. 94 1-8
Science	Pg. 54-59 exer. Pg. 61-66 NH	Pg. 54-59 exer. Pg. 61-66 D.	rd. Pg. 61-66 exer. Pg. 67 1-5 D.	rd. Pg. 67-73 exer. Pg. 76 1-6 D.	NH
Tests & Reports	NH	Prac. test, Wed	chapter 2 on friday	review friday Quiz	Science test

Completing Your Personal Assignment Sheet

Perhaps you believe that you already have a good system for recording your assignments. One of your teachers or your resource specialist may have already taught you a good method. Some teachers do all the work for you. Each week they give students a completed weekly assignment sheet, and you do not have to write down your assignments. Some schools have an "official" homework-recording system that all students are required to use. If your school or teacher has one, then, of course, you should continue using it.

It is also possible that you bought an assignment book that you like in a store. Perhaps you have created your own method for recording homework and feel that it works very well for you.

Even though you may already have a good method, it can be useful to experiment with new ways to do things. With your teachers' permission, use the assignment sheets in this book for a couple of weeks. You may discover that you like this new system better than the one you are currently using. If you don't like the system and you conclude your old method works better for you, you can always go back to using it.

On page 32, you will find an assignment sheet exactly like the Practice Assignment Sheet that you've already completed. You will note that the subjects have not been included, as students do not necessarily take the same classes. Fill in the subjects you are taking on the assignment sheet. You can fill in as many as four classes. If you are taking more than four classes that assign homework, you may need to modify the assignment sheet. Your teacher can show you how.

Begin to use the assignment sheet today as an experiment. If you have already written down your assignments using your old method, transfer the information to this sheet. Make sure to write down all the important details. Forgetting to indicate that there is an important math test on Wednesday could be a disaster!

My Personal Assignment Sheet

SUBJECTS	MONDAY	TUESDAY	WEDNESDAY	THURSDAY	FRIDAY
__________					
__________					
__________					
__________					
Tests & Reports					

Using an assignment sheet can help you get organized and reduce stress. If you carefully fill in the important information, the assignment sheet guarantees that you will know what the teacher expects from you and will prevent you from getting confused about what to do each evening.

There is another very important consideration if you want your assignment-recording system to work for you. You must write neatly. No homework-recording system will work if you cannot read what you write!

Each assignment sheet can be used for only one week. Your teacher may have extra photocopied assignment sheets that you can use in the weeks ahead. Make sure to use a divider in the front of your binder that is labeled "Assignments." Punch holes in your assignment sheets and put them in this section. This way you will always know what your homework is as soon as you open your binder.

Remember to get in the habit of recording your assignments on the sheet each day. This may seem like extra work, but before long you will be using the system without even having to think about. It will make your life much easier. Mom's too!

Now that you have learned in Unit 1 how to organize your time and you have learned in this unit how to record your assignments properly, the next step is to learn how to organize your materials. This will be covered in Unit 3.

What I Have Learned about Recording Assignments

Circle **True** or **False:**

If you have a good memory, you do not need an assignment sheet.	**True False**
When writing down your assignments, you should always indicate when there is a test scheduled and a report or essay is due.	**True False**
You should place your assignment sheet in the front of your binder.	**True False**
You only need to use an assignment sheet when there's a lot of homework.	**True False**
You should write down the teacher's clues about tests or about how to complete an assignment on another piece of paper, if it won't fit on your assignment sheet.	**True False**
You should never use abbreviations.	**True False**
Teachers always write assignments on the chalkboard.	**True False**
You should look at your assignment sheet every evening before starting your homework.	**True False**
One good way to avoid having to write down assignments is to call a friend and ask what the homework is.	**True False**
You should put down as few details as possible when recording your assignments.	**True False**
On days when only one or two teachers have assigned homework, you do not need to write down your assignments. You can remember them.	**True False**

Unit 3

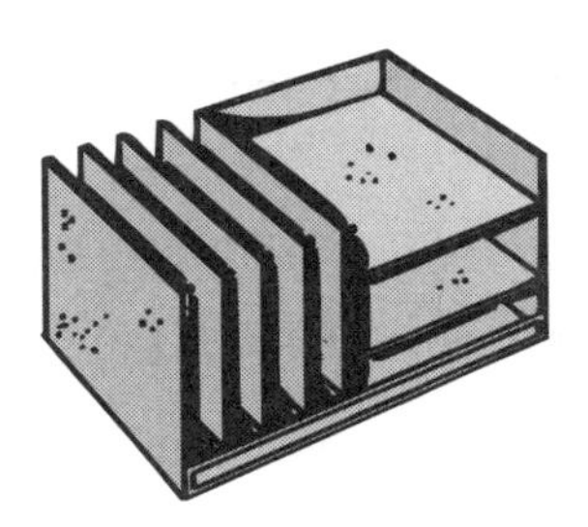

Organizing Your Study Materials

Having the Tools to Do the Job

After some heavy-duty coaxing from his mother, Justin finally went to his room to start his homework. He always tried to put it off until the last minute, partially from habit and partially because he found some of the work quite difficult and demanding.

Justin had to admit that he was making progress in school. Reading and math were easier, and the techniques he had learned in the resource program for identifying, understanding, and remembering key information in his textbooks made studying less painful. Learning how to record his assignments accurately and learning how to become better organized had also been a big help. Still, procrastination was a hard-to-break habit.

Justin sighed as he sat down at his desk and turned on his desk lamp. He knew he couldn't put off doing his homework any longer. Reaching into his book bag, he pulled out his social studies textbook. Justin could always tell which one it was without even looking. It was the biggest and the heaviest book in the bag.

Justin now pulled his binder out of his book bag. Turning to his weekly assignment page in the first section of his binder, he looked at the homework that was due the next day. He had assignments in math, social studies, and science. Fortunately, he has already completed his English assignment in school. He had also completed half of his math assignment in the resource room.

Justin quickly scanned down to the bottom of the page to see if there were any tests or reports due later in the week. He noted that there would be a science quiz on Friday, and his book report was due in ten days. Justin was glad that he had already read half the book. He planned on completing the second half over the weekend, and he would begin writing the book report on Sunday. That would give him enough time to finish it on Tuesday, proofread and recopy it on Wednesday, and submit it when it was due on Thursday.

After reviewing his assignments for the week, Justin checked his study schedule. It was taped on the wall in front of his desk. Justin was fairly certain he could do all of his homework in the time he had budgeted.

Justin's history assignment was to read pages 71 - 76 in Chapter 4. He then had to answer questions 1 through 6 at the end of the chapter. On his assignment sheet, he had written: "p. 71 – 76 Ch. 4. Ques. 1 – 6 p. 87. Cmplt. sen. Skip line btwn ans." Justin spent the next fifteen minutes reading the assigned pages. He then reached for some loose-leaf paper on the shelf above his desk. He skipped to the questions at the end of the chapter, took a pen out of the desk drawer, and began to answer the questions. He made certain that he wrote complete sentences that contained a subject and a verb, and he also made certain that he skipped a line between each answer. It took Justin fifteen minutes to answer the questions and proofread his answers to make sure he hadn't made any careless mistakes. When he was finished, he took a ten-minute cookies-and-milk break in the kitchen.

Justin's language arts assignment was to look up eight words in the dictionary, write the definitions, and use each word in a sentence that showed that he understood the meaning of the word. On a second piece of paper, Justin wrote his name and the date at the top as the teacher had instructed. He reached for his dictionary and began to look up the first word. When he found the word he was looking for, he wrote down the definition. Then he wrote a sentence using the word and underlined the word in the sentence. He followed this procedure with the other seven words the teacher had assigned.

Justin worked for twenty-five minutes, and then he took a five-minute break. He wandered into the living room where his father was reading the newspaper. They spoke briefly about how the Green Bay Packers and the Boston Patriots were doing. Green Bay was Justin's favorite team. His father, having grown up in Boston, was a staunch Patriots fan, and this led to many heated, but good-natured, arguments.

After the brief visit, Justin returned to his room to finish his math homework. When the math was finished, he started to read the assigned pages in his science textbook. He then turned to page 87 and began to memorize the assigned chemistry formulas. He wrote NaCl on an index card and under it he wrote sodium chloride. In parenthesis he wrote table salt. He did the same thing with HCl (hydrochloric acid), H_2SO_4 (sulfuric acid) and $HN0_3$ (nitric acid). Using felt pens that he kept in his desk drawer, he wrote each formula in a different color. Then he closed his eyes and tried to see the formula and the description in the color he had chosen. His resource specialist had taught him this trick, and Justin found that it helped him memorize information.

Justin's homework was almost finished. He had worked for an hour and thirty minutes. All he had to do was begin reviewing for the science quiz. He estimated that this would take about twenty-five minutes. Dinner was in fifteen minutes. Justin planned on reviewing his science notes after dinner. Then he would have time to watch TV, e-mail some of his friends, and play a video game. He would have two whole hours of free time before bed.

Examining Someone Else's Study Procedure

The description of how Justin studies provides you with clues about what kind of student he is. The story also describes the specific procedures he followed for organizing himself.

Go back to the story and see how many of Justin's study procedures you can identify. Underline each of the procedures and then number them in the order in which they occurred. (*Clue*: There are approximately 39 specific actions or procedures. You may find less if you combine two separate actions that are described in the same sentence. If you can find 35 or more, you have done a great job!) When you are done, compare what you were able to identify with the procedures that are identified and numbered below.

Identifying the Specifics of Justin's Study Procedure

After some heavy-duty coaxing from his mother, Justin finally went to his room to start his homework.**1** He always tried to put it off to the last minute,**2** partially from habit and partially because he found some of the work quite difficult and demanding.

Justin had to admit that he was making progress in school. Reading and math were easier, and the techniques he had learned in the resource program for identifying, understanding, and remembering key information in his textbooks made studying less painful. Learning how to record his assignments accurately and learning how to become better organized had also been a big help. Still, procrastination was a hard-to-break habit.

<u>Justin sighed as he sat down at his desk and turned on his desk lamp</u>.**3** He knew he couldn't put off doing his homework any longer. <u>Reaching into his book bag, he pulled out his social studies textbook.</u>**4** Justin could always tell which one it was without even looking. It was the biggest and the heaviest book in the bag.

<u>Justin now pulled his binder out of his book bag</u>. **5** <u>Turning to his weekly assignment page in the first section of his binder, he looked at the homework that was due the next day</u>. **6** He had assignments in math, social studies, and science. Fortunately, <u>he has already completed his entire English assignment in school</u>. **7** <u>He had also completed half of his math assignment in the resource room</u>. **8**

<u>Justin quickly scanned down to the bottom of the page to see if there were any tests or reports due later in the week</u>.**9** He noted that there would be a science quiz on Friday, and his book report was due in ten days. Justin was glad that he had already read half the book. <u>He planned on reading the second half of the book over the weekend</u>, **10** and <u>he would begin writing the report on Sunday</u>.**11** That would give him enough time to <u>finish writing the report on Monday and Tuesday</u>, **12** <u>proofread and recopy it on Wednesday</u>, **13** and <u>submit it on time on Thursday</u>.**14**

<u>After reviewing his assignments for the week, Justin checked his study schedule</u>.**15** <u>It was taped on the wall in front of his desk</u>. **16** Justin was fairly certain he could do all of his homework in the time he had budgeted.

Justin's history assignment was to read pages 71 - 76 in Chapter 4. He then had to answer questions 1 through 6 at the end of the chapter. <u>On his assignment sheet, he had written: "p. 71 – 76 Ch. 4. Ques. 1 – 6 p. 87. Cmplt. sen. Skip line btwn ans."</u>**17** <u>Justin spent the next fifteen minutes reading the assigned pages</u>.**18** <u>He then reached for some loose-leaf paper on the shelf above his desk.</u>**19** <u>He skipped to questions at the end of the chapter, took a pen out of the desk drawer, and began to answer the questions</u>.**20** <u>He made certain that he wrote complete sentences that contained a subject and a verb</u>,**21** <u>and he also made certain that he skipped a line between each answer</u>.**22** <u>It took Justin fifteen minutes to answer the questions and proofread his answers to make sure he hadn't made any careless mistakes</u>. **23** <u>When he was finished, he took a ten-minute cookies-and-milk break in the kitchen.</u>**24**

Justin's language arts assignment was to look up eight words in the dictionary, write the definitions, and use each word in a sentence that showed that he understood the meaning of the word. On a second piece of paper, Justin wrote his name and the date at the top as the teacher had instructed.**25** He reached for his dictionary and began to look up the first word.**26** When he found the word he was looking for, he wrote down the definition.**27** Then he wrote a sentence using the word and underlined the word in the sentence.**28** He followed this procedure with the other seven words the teacher had assigned. **29**

Justin worked for twenty-five minutes, and then he took a five-minute break. **30** He wandered into the living room where his father was reading the newspaper. They spoke briefly about how the Green Bay Packers and the Boston Patriots were doing. Green Bay was Justin's favorite team. His father, having grown up in Boston, was a staunch Patriots fan, and this led to many heated, but always good-natured, arguments.

After the brief visit, Justin returned to his room to finish his math homework.**31** When he was finished, he started to read the assigned pages in his science textbook.**32** He then turned to page 87 and began to memorize the assigned chemistry formulas.**33** He wrote NaCl on an index card and under it he wrote sodium chloride.**34** In parenthesis he wrote table salt.**35** He did the same thing with HCl (hydrochloric acid), H_2SO_4 (sulfuric acid) and $HN0_3$ (nitric acid). **36** Using felt pens that he kept in his desk drawer, he wrote each formula in a different color.**37** Then he closed his eyes and tried to see the formula and the description in the color he had chosen. **38** His resource specialist had taught him this trick, and Justin found that it helped him memorize information.

Justin's homework was almost finished. He had worked for an hour and thirty minutes. All he had left to do was begin reviewing for the science quiz. He estimated that this would take about twenty-five minutes. Dinner was in fifteen minutes. Justin planned on reviewing his science notes after dinner. **39** Then he would have time to watch TV, e-mail some of his friends, and play a video game. He would have two whole hours of free time before bed.

Evaluating Another Person's Study Style

How would you evaluate Justin's decision to do his homework sitting at a desk?

1 2 3 4 5 6 7 8 9 10

Not Smart **Fairly Smart** **Very Smart**

How would you evaluate Justin's habit of putting off doing his homework for a long as possible?

1 2 3 4 5 6 7 8 9 10

Not Smart **Fairly Smart** **Very Smart**

How would you evaluate Justin having at hand all the materials he needed to do his homework?

1 2 3 4 5 6 7 8 9 10

Not Smart **Fairly Smart** **Very Smart**

How would you evaluate Justin's decision to tape his schedule on the wall in front of his desk?

1 2 3 4 5 6 7 8 9 10

Not Smart **Fairly Smart** **Very Smart**

How would you evaluate Justin's decision to have an assignment sheet?

1 2 3 4 5 6 7 8 9 10

Not Smart **Fairly Smart** **Very Smart**

How would you evaluate Justin's overall study procedure?

1 2 3 4 5 6 7 8 9 10

Not Smart **Fairly Smart** **Very Smart**

Predicting What Will Happen

Based upon Justin's behavior, you should be able to make some predictions about the consequences of his study procedure.

His grades in school:

1 2 3 4 5 6 7 8 9 10 ***Possible*** ***Probable***

Poor **Average** **Excellent**

His relationship with his parents:

1 2 3 4 5 6 7 8 9 10 ***Possible*** ***Probable***

Poor **Average** **Excellent**

His relationship with his teacher:

1 2 3 4 5 6 7 8 9 10 *Possible* *Probable*

Poor Average Excellent

His self-confidence in school:

1 2 3 4 5 6 7 8 9 10 *Possible* *Probable*

Poor Average Excellent

Can you think of any additional steps Justin might take that could further improve his organization or grades? If so, list them below.

1. ____

2. ____

3. ____

Why Create a Personal Organization System?

Perhaps you are thinking: "I'm not sure if I want to be as organized as Justin. It seems like it would take too much work."

Actually, becoming organized requires *less* work in the long run! Once you create an effective organizational system, you will spend much less time looking for the things you need to do your work. You'll know what your assignments are, and you'll know where your books, binder, dictionary, paper, and pencils are. Because you are working more efficiently, studying will be easier, and you can spend the time you save doing things you enjoy.

Making Certain You Have the Necessary Materials

Imagine sitting down to do your science homework assignment and discovering that you left your science textbook in school. Imagine not having any loose-leaf paper or a pen. Imagine not having a dictionary at home when your English assignment is to look up ten vocabulary words.

If you get in the habit of using the three *checklists*, you cannot help but become more organized.

Checklist #1: Materials and supplies you need to take home every day.

Checklist #2: Materials and supplies you need to take to school in the morning.

Checklist #3: Materials you need in your study area at home to do your work.

The checklists do not have to be complicated. Let's take a look what they might look like.

Checklist #1 -- Materials to Bring Home

	Mon.	Tues.	Wed.	Thurs.	Fri.
Binder	____	____	____	____	____
Textbooks	____	____	____	____	____
Assignment Sheet	____	____	____	____	____
Workbooks	____	____	____	____	____
Handouts	____	____	____	____	____
Study Guides	____	____	____	____	____
Corrected Assignments	____	____	____	____	____
Graded Tests	____	____	____	____	____
______________________	____	____	____	____	____
______________________	____	____	____	____	____
______________________	____	____	____	____	____
______________________	____	____	____	____	____

Checklist #2 -- Materials to Bring to School

	Mon.	Tues.	Wed.	Thurs.	Fri.
Binder	____	____	____	____	____
Textbooks	____	____	____	____	____
Assignment Sheet	____	____	____	____	____
Workbooks	____	____	____	____	____
Study Guides	____	____	____	____	____
Completed Homework	____	____	____	____	____
Paper	____	____	____	____	____
Pencils and Pens	____	____	____	____	____
______________________	____	____	____	____	____
______________________	____	____	____	____	____
______________________	____	____	____	____	____
______________________	____	____	____	____	____

Checklist #3 -- Home Study Environment

	Mon.	Tues.	Wed.	Thurs.	Fri.
Quiet Study Area	____	____	____	____	____
Desk or Table	____	____	____	____	____
Dictionary	____	____	____	____	____
Paper	____	____	____	____	____
Pencils and Pens	____	____	____	____	____
Ruler	____	____	____	____	____
Books and Study Materials	____	____	____	____	____
______________________	____	____	____	____	____
______________________	____	____	____	____	____
______________________	____	____	____	____	____
______________________	____	____	____	____	____

Begin by actually checking off each item on the list. Because the checklists are so simple, they will only take a few seconds to complete. Start out by actually checking off each item on the list. Before long, you'll be able to check the items off *in your mind.* After using the checklists a few times, running through them every day will quickly become a habit. The goal is to make the procedure of going through the checklists automatic.

As you can see, there are several blank spaces at the end of each checklist. Write in these spaces any special materials or supplies you might need such as a ruler, calculator, compass, or highlighting pens.

For the next week try an experiment. Check off each item on the checklist for every school day. Getting organized and having the materials you need to do your homework can be easy once you develop the habit!

Organizing Your Binder

Perhaps you have already organized your binder so that you can find everything you need to do your work efficiently. If you have organized your binder, check off the following steps to make sure you have done it properly. If your binder is not already properly organized, go through the steps *carefully*.

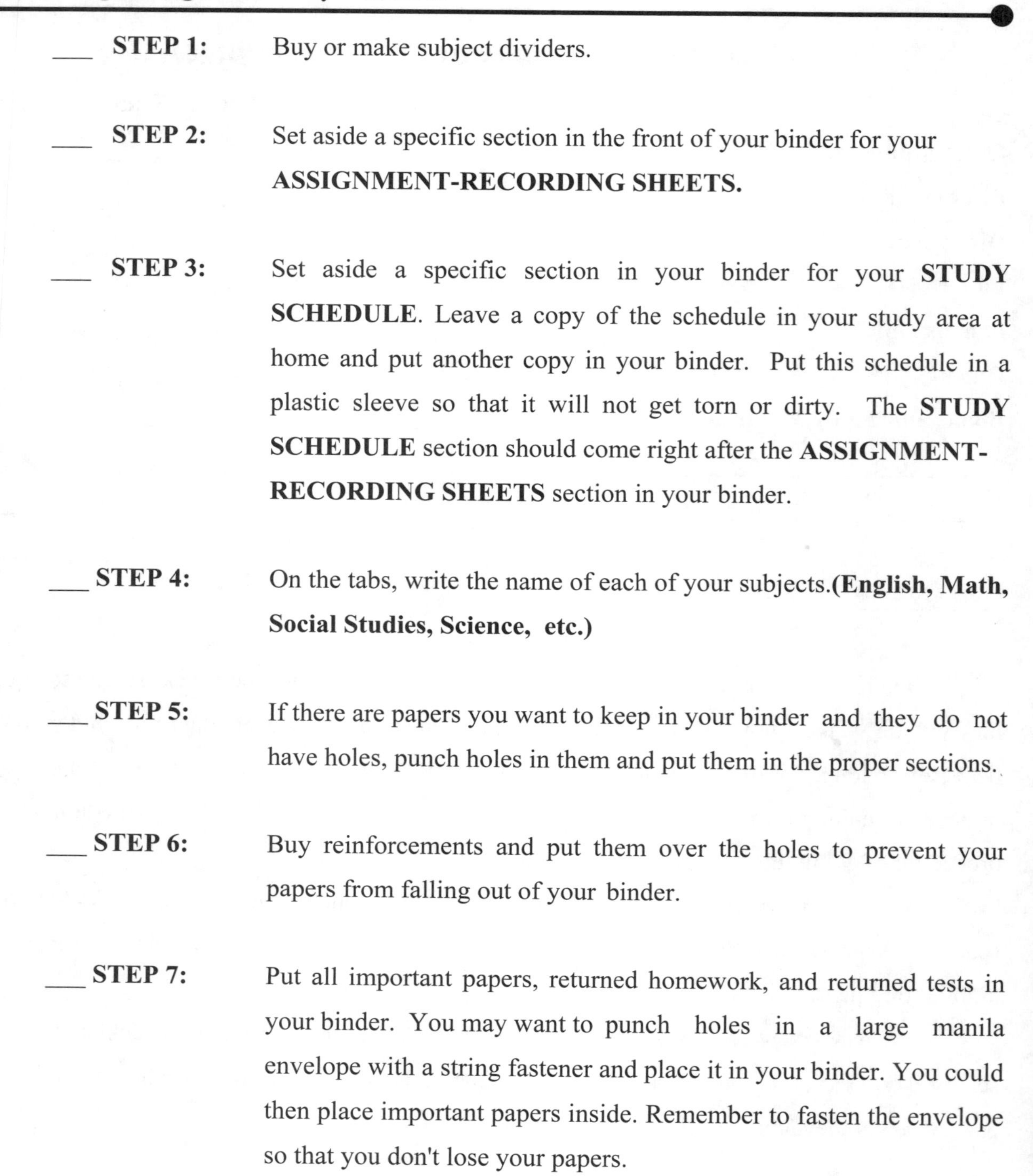

___ **STEP 1:** Buy or make subject dividers.

___ **STEP 2:** Set aside a specific section in the front of your binder for your **ASSIGNMENT-RECORDING SHEETS.**

___ **STEP 3:** Set aside a specific section in your binder for your **STUDY SCHEDULE**. Leave a copy of the schedule in your study area at home and put another copy in your binder. Put this schedule in a plastic sleeve so that it will not get torn or dirty. The **STUDY SCHEDULE** section should come right after the **ASSIGNMENT-RECORDING SHEETS** section in your binder.

___ **STEP 4:** On the tabs, write the name of each of your subjects.**(English, Math, Social Studies, Science, etc.)**

___ **STEP 5:** If there are papers you want to keep in your binder and they do not have holes, punch holes in them and put them in the proper sections.

___ **STEP 6:** Buy reinforcements and put them over the holes to prevent your papers from falling out of your binder.

___ **STEP 7:** Put all important papers, returned homework, and returned tests in your binder. You may want to punch holes in a large manila envelope with a string fastener and place it in your binder. You could then place important papers inside. Remember to fasten the envelope so that you don't lose your papers.

Students who think strategically will take the time to complete these steps. The entire procedure shouldn't take more than an hour. If you need help, ask your teacher or your parent. Once you have organized your binder, you'll be very thankful. Students who know where to find their important papers will spend less time searching for what they need. This will make their lives and their studying much easier.

What I Have Learned about Organizing Materials

1. Students with good memories don't need to worry about organization. **True** **False**

2. Being organized takes too much time. **True** **False**

3. Being organized will save you time in the long run. **True** **False**

4. Putting dividers in your binder will help you locate papers more easily. **True** **False**

5. It doesn't matter where you write down your assignments as long as you write them down somewhere. **True** **False**

6. Using checklists to help you remember is dumb. **True** **False**

7. You can always find the materials you need to do your homework even if you're not well-organized. **True** **False**

8. If you forget to bring home something from school, you can always ask your parents to drive you back to school to get it. **True** **False**

9. Once the necessary supplies checklists become a habit, you can run through the list in your mind. **True** **False**

10. You don't need to organize your binder. Just stuff your papers in your backpack. **True** **False**

11 You don't need to worry about getting organized until you are in 10th grade. **True** **False**

12. There's no link between getting good grades and being organized. **True** **False**

13. There's plenty of time to become organized when you become an adult. **True** **False**

14. It is more fun to be disorganized **True** **False**

Unit 4

Creating the Best Study Environment

Operating Below Peak Performance

Kenesha was lying on the carpet in the living room. Her head was cradled in the palms of her hands, and her history textbook and binder were lying on the floor in front of her. She had positioned herself in front of the TV which she had tuned to her favorite channel. She had set the volume on high so that she could hear the TV despite the loud background noise in the room. While she was working, her younger brother was playing a space-alien game on the family computer that was on a table on the other side of the room. Every few seconds the sound of an exploding space ship would blast from the computer, and her brother would scream with delight as his score flashed on the screen.

After reading through the assigned pages in the textbook, Kenesha pulled her binder closer and began answering the questions at the end of the chapter. If she couldn't answer a question, she would turn back to the chapter to find the information. From time to time, she would stop what she was doing and glance up at the TV and smile or laugh out loud. Her favorite sitcom was on, and she never missed an episode.

Examining How Someone Else Studies

The description of Kenesha's studying environment provides you with clues about how she does her homework.

Go back into the story. Number each of Kenesha's behaviors, and highlight each behavior using one color. (If you prefer, you can use colored pencils instead of a highlighter.) Then number and use a different color to highlight each event that is going on around her as she studies. (*Clue #1*: **Eleven** specific behaviors are described. In some cases, more than one behavior is described in a particular sentence. *Clue #2:* **Five** specific events are going on in the environment around her. See if you can find them all.) When you have finished, compare what you were able to identify with the procedures that are identified and numbered below.

Identifying the Specifics

Kenesha was lying on the carpet in the living room. **1.** Her head was cradled in the palms of her hands, **2** and her science textbook and binder were lying on the floor in front of her.**3** . She had positioned herself in front of the TV **4** that she had tuned to her favorite channel.**5** She had set the volume on high **6** so she could hear the TV despite **the loud background noise in the room.1** While she was working, **her younger brother was playing a space-alien game on the family computer 2 that was on a table on the other side of the room. 3 Every few seconds the sound of an exploding space ship would blast from the computer,4 and her brother would scream with delight as his score flashed on the screen. 5**

After reading through the assigned pages in the textbook, **7** Kenesha pulled her binder closer and began answering the questions at the end of the chapter. **8** If she couldn't answer a question, she would turn back to the chapter to find the information **.9** From time to time, Kenesha would stop what she was doing and glance up at the TV. **10** Her favorite sitcom was on, and she never missed an episode. **11**

Evaluating the Identified Study Procedures

How would you evaluate Kenesha's decision to do her homework while lying on the floor in the living room?

1 2 3 4 5 6 7 8 9 10

Not Smart **Fairly Smart** **Very Smart**

How would you evaluate Kenesha's decision to watch her favorite sitcom while doing her homework?

1 2 3 4 5 6 7 8 9 10

Not Smart **Fairly Smart** **Very Smart**

How would you evaluate Kenesha's overall study procedure?

1 2 3 4 5 6 7 8 9 10

Not Smart **Fairly Smart** **Very Smart**

Predicting What Will Happen

Make some predictions about the consequences of Kenesha's study style.

Her ability to concentrate:

1 2 3 4 5 6 7 8 9 10 ***Possible*** ***Probable***

Poor **Average** **Excellent**

Her grades:

1 2 3 4 5 6 7 8 9 10 ***Possible*** ***Probable***

Poor **Average** **Excellent**

Her parents' attitude about the way she studies:

1 2 3 4 5 6 7 8 9 10 ***Possible*** ***Probable***

Not Critical **Somewhat Critical** **Extremely Critical**

Her teachers' attitudes about the way she studies:

1 2 3 4 5 6 7 8 9 10 ***Possible*** ***Probable***

Not Critical **Somewhat Critical** **Extremely Critical**

Defending a Position

Write down some reasons that Kenesha would probably give to justify her studying style.

1. ____

____

2. ____

____

3. ____

____

Imagine that Kenesha's parents are unhappy with how she does her homework. Why would they be concerned? ____

____

____

What do you think they would say to her? ____

____

____

How do you think Kenesha would respond to their concerns? ____

____

____

Let's say Kenesha argues that there's nothing wrong with her studying procedure. Do you agree?

____

Why? ____

____

Do you think that Kenesha's parents are nagging her and should leave her alone? **Yes** **No**

If you were Kenesha's friend, what specific recommendations might you make to her that could improve her study environment and learning efficiency?

1. ____
2. ____
3. ____
4. ____
5. ____

Doing Several Things at Once

What do you think would happen if....?

You try to watch two soccer games at the same time.

Consequence: ____

Possible **Probable**

You are at a party and you are trying to listen to three friends who are all talking at the same time.

Consequence: ____

Possible **Probable**

You try to set your watch while taking a test.

Consequence: ____

Possible **Probable**

You try to study while playing a computer game.

Consequence: ____

Possible **Probable**

You try to do your math homework while having an argument with your sister.

Consequence: ____

Possible **Probable**

You try to kick a goal while waving at your friends on the sidelines.

Consequence: ____

Possible **Probable**

You take a test while glancing at a comic book that you have put in your lap.

Consequence: ____

Possible **Probable**

You try to drill holes and saw wood while watching television.

Consequence: ____

Possible **Probable**

Do you believe that you can do more than one thing at a time? You may be thinking: "Well, sometimes I can!" Under certain circumstances, it is possible to do several things at once. For example, you could talk to a friend while you are both riding your bikes or tossing a football. If, however, you are on the basketball court playing a game, you would need to concentrate on what you are doing. Imagine talking to a friend while you're making a lay-up or when you are shooting a jump shot! If you're shooting a foul shot while you're wondering about what you are going to have for dinner, there's a good chance that you'll miss the shot.

You may have a good brain, but even a good brain can only devote 100% of its attention to one thing at a time. In many respects, studying is like playing a sport. To play at peak performance, you must focus exclusively on what you are doing.

Evaluate the following situations:

Studying for a test while listening to loud music

1 2 3 4 5 6 7 8 9 10

Not Smart **Fairly Smart** **Very Smart**

Lying on your bed while writing a book report

1 2 3 4 5 6 7 8 9 10

Not Smart **Fairly Smart** **Very Smart**

Doing your math homework while sitting at a desk

1 2 3 4 5 6 7 8 9 10

Not Smart **Fairly Smart** **Very Smart**

Not answering the telephone when you're studying

1 2 3 4 5 6 7 8 9 10

Not Smart **Fairly Smart** **Very Smart**

Fooling around with things on your desk while you are studying

1 2 3 4 5 6 7 8 9 10

Not Smart **Fairly Smart** **Very Smart**

Focusing for a minimum of twenty minutes when doing homework before you take a study break

1	2	3	4	5	6	7	8	9	10
Not Smart			**Fairly Smart**					**Very Smart**	

Creating Your Own Study Fortress

To help you focus and work more efficiently when you study, you might want to create a study fortress in your mind. The fortress is peaceful, well-organized, and well-protected. You are sitting at a desk or table at the center of the fortress. You have everything you need to do your work: good light, necessary supplies, books, binder, assignment sheet, and study schedule. Your fortress is quiet, and you have intentionally eliminated distractions so you that can concentrate and study efficiently. Once you finish your homework or take a well-deserved break, you can walk away from your fortress and "return to civilization." If there's still more to do after your break, you can simply head back to the fortress, close the door, and begin studying again.

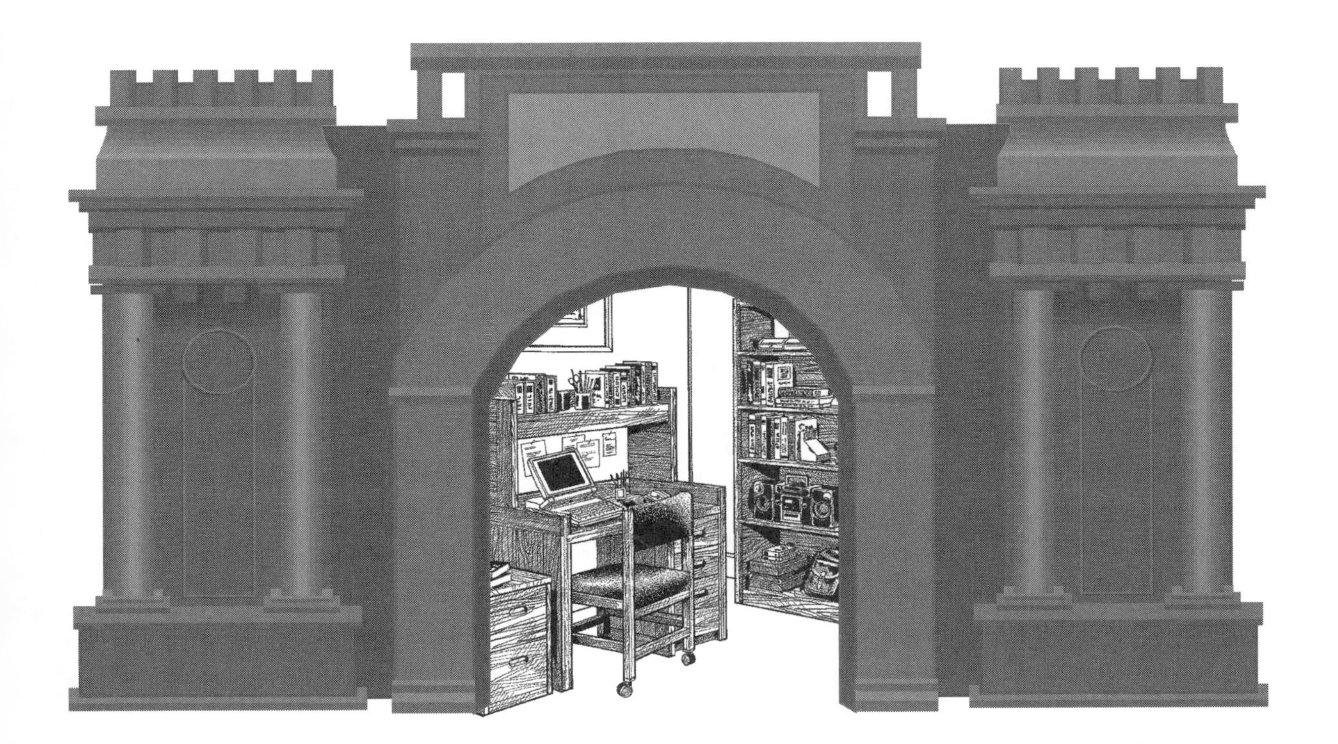

What's Right in This Picture?

Describe all of the details that you see in this illustration that would enhance effective studying.

1. ______________________________
2. ______________________________
3. ______________________________
4. ______________________________
5. ______________________________
6. ______________________________
7. ______________________________

Make some predictions about studying in the study environment shown in the illustration. Circle the number that corresponds to your prediction and indicate whether the prediction is possible or probable.

The quality of the student's work:

1 2 3 4 5 6 7 8 9 10 ***Possible Probable***

Poor Average Excellent

Why did you make this evaluation?

____

____

____

The quality of the student's concentration:

1 2 3 4 5 6 7 8 9 10 ***Possible Probable***

Poor Average Excellent

Why did you make this evaluation?

____

____

____

The quality of the student's grades:

1 2 3 4 5 6 7 8 9 10 ***Possible Probable***

Poor Average Excellent

Why did you make this evaluation?

____

____

____

What's Wrong in This Picture?

Identify as many conditions in the picture as you can that might interfere with effective studying.

1. ____________________
2. ____________________
3. ____________________
4. ____________________
5. ____________________
6. ____________________
7. ____________________

Make some predictions about studying in the study environment shown in the illustration. Circle the number that corresponds to your prediction and indicate whether the prediction is possible or probable.

The quality of the student's work:

1 2 3 4 5 6 7 8 9 10 ***Possible Probable***

Poor Average Excellent

The quality of the student's concentration:

1 2 3 4 5 6 7 8 9 10 ***Possible Probable***

Poor Average Excellent

The quality of the student's grades:

1 2 3 4 5 6 7 8 9 10 ***Possible Probable***

Poor Average Excellent

Ideas for Reducing Distractions When You Study

Make a list of the specific steps you could take to reduce distractions in your own study environment. For example, your list might include:

- No TV or radio while studying
- No conversations while studying
- Studying at a desk
- Studying or doing homework for a minimum of 20 minutes before taking a break

Ways to Reduce Distractions When I Study

1. ____________________
2. ____________________
3. ____________________
4. ____________________
5. ____________________
6. ____________________
7. ____________________

Experimenting with Reducing Distractions

It is time to try an experiment using your ideas for reducing distractions. Carefully follow your *studying more efficiently* guidelines for two weeks. Make your best effort during the experiment and use the guidelines consistently. If you discover that your schoolwork has improved, you'll know that your study environment does, in fact, affect your performance. It would certainly make sense for you to incorporate the guidelines into your study procedures. During the experiment, you can use the following chart to record your grades on homework assignments and tests. Record your performance in each of your subjects. When your graded homework is returned, write down the grade or number of correct or incorrect answers. In this way you can compare how you are doing as you work to improve your study procedures.

Keeping Track of My Performance During the Experiment

Subject: ________________

Homework:

Date:_______ **Grade:______** **Date:______** **Grade:_______**

Date:_______ **Grade:______** **Date:______** **Grade:_______**

Date:_______ **Grade:______** **Date:______** **Grade:_______**

Date:_______ **Grade:______** **Date:______** **Grade:_______**

Date:_______ **Grade:______** **Date:______** **Grade:_______**

Tests:

Date:_______ **Grade:______** **Date:______** **Grade:_______**

Date:_______ **Grade:______** **Date:______** **Grade:_______**

Date:_______ **Grade:______** **Date:______** **Grade:_______**

Subject: ________________

Homework:

Date:_______ Grade:______ Date:______ Grade:_______

Date:_______ Grade:______ Date:______ Grade:_______

Date:_______ Grade:______ Date:______ Grade:_______

Date:_______ Grade:______ Date:______ Grade:_______

Date:_______ Grade:______ Date:______ Grade:_______

Tests:

Date:_______ Grade:______ Date:______ Grade:_______

Date:_______ Grade:______ Date:______ Grade:_______

Date:_______ Grade:______ Date:______ Grade:_______

Subject: ________________

Homework:

Date:_______ Grade:______ Date:______ Grade:_______

Date:_______ Grade:______ Date:______ Grade:_______

Date:_______ Grade:______ Date:______ Grade:_______

Date:_______ Grade:______ Date:______ Grade:_______

Date:_______ Grade:______ Date:______ Grade:_______

Tests:

Date:_______ Grade:______ Date:______ Grade:_______

Date:_______ Grade:______ Date:______ Grade:_______

Date:_______ Grade:______ Date:______ Grade:_______

Subject: ________________

Homework:

Date:_______	**Grade:______**	**Date:______**	**Grade:_______**
Date:_______	**Grade:______**	**Date:______**	**Grade:_______**
Date:_______	**Grade:______**	**Date:______**	**Grade:_______**
Date:_______	**Grade:______**	**Date:______**	**Grade:_______**
Date:_______	**Grade:______**	**Date:______**	**Grade:_______**

Tests:

Date:_______	**Grade:______**	**Date:______**	**Grade:_______**
Date:_______	**Grade:______**	**Date:______**	**Grade:_______**
Date:_______	**Grade:______**	**Date:______**	**Grade:_______**

Subject: ________________

Homework:

Date:_______	**Grade:______**	**Date:______**	**Grade:_______**
Date:_______	**Grade:______**	**Date:______**	**Grade:_______**
Date:_______	**Grade:______**	**Date:______**	**Grade:_______**
Date:_______	**Grade:______**	**Date:______**	**Grade:_______**
Date:_______	**Grade:______**	**Date:______**	**Grade:_______**

Tests:

Date:_______	**Grade:______**	**Date:______**	**Grade:_______**
Date:_______	**Grade:______**	**Date:______**	**Grade:_______**
Date:_______	**Grade:______**	**Date:______**	**Grade:_______**

Plotting Your Progress

You can use the information about your grades to plot your performance on a chart. This will provide a quick overview of your progress. On the next page is an example of how the chart might look.

Sample Performance Chart
Homework Results

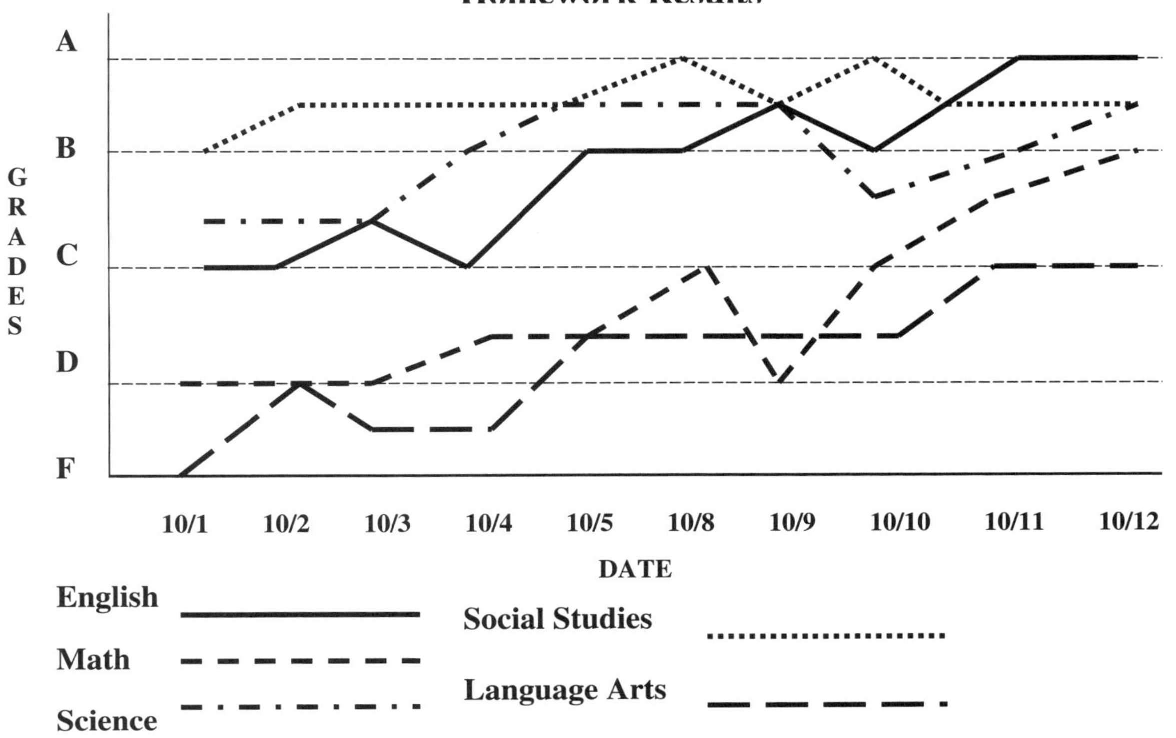

Sample Performance Chart
Test Results

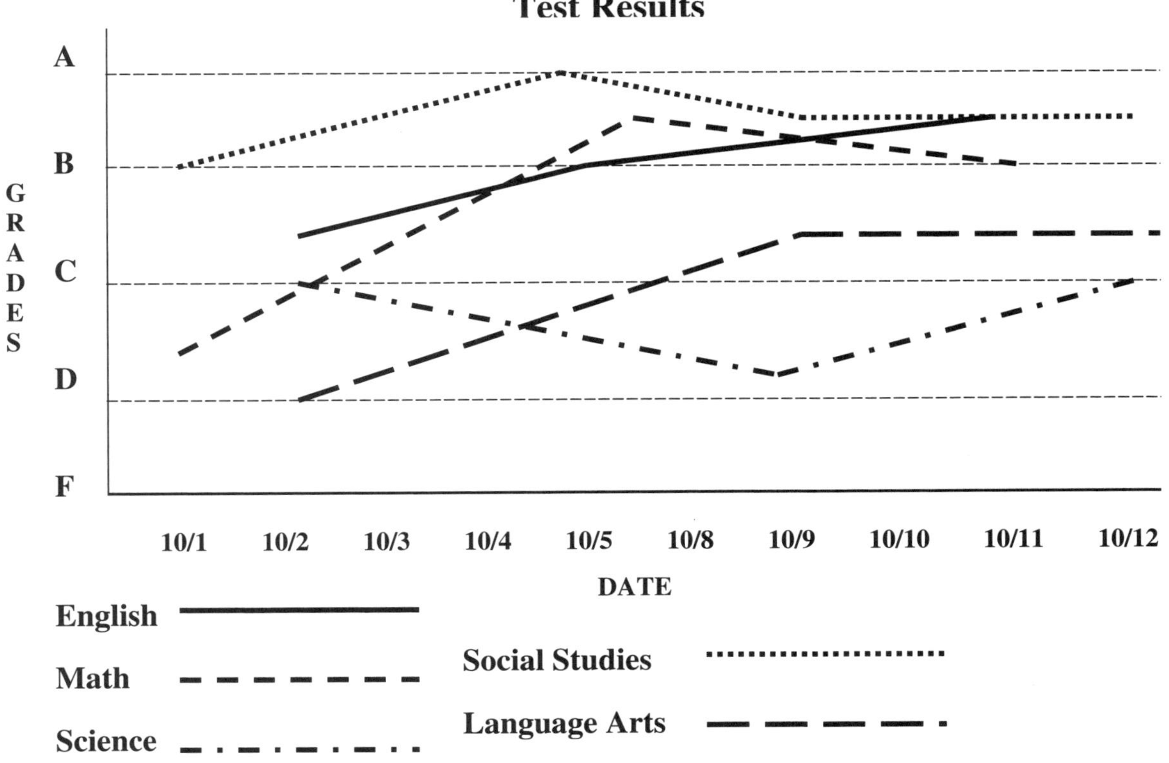

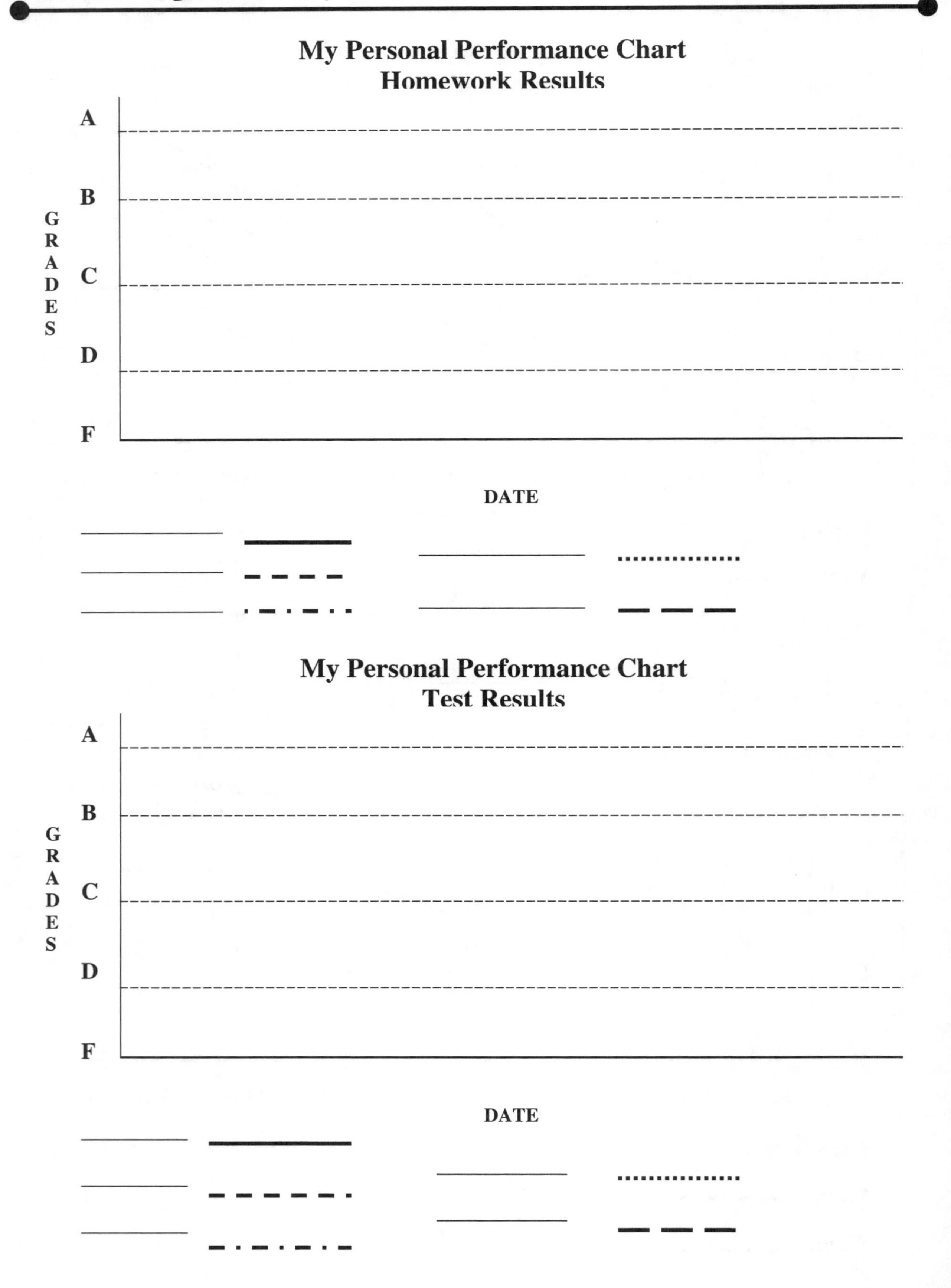
My Personal Performance Chart
Homework Results
A
B
C
D
F
GRADES
DATE
My Personal Performance Chart
Test Results
A
B
C
D
F
GRADES
DATE

The preceding performance chart can accommodate data about one week's performance. You will want to photocopy the form so that you can plot your performance for at least two weeks. Once you have put in the information, you will be able to see at a glance how you are doing in each of your subjects.

What I Have Learned about My Study Environment

Match the following causes (actions) with the likely consequences. Many of the consequences can be linked to more than one cause. Find as many links as you can.

Watching TV while doing homework
Listening to loud music while studying
Studying lying on the floor
Talking on the phone while studying
Leaving work until the last minute
Doing homework during TV commercials
Doing math and reading homework at the same time
Studying in a noisy place
Studying while thinking about other things
Taking breaks every few minutes
Fooling around with things on the desk
Listening to conversations in another room

Doing sloppy work
Becoming distracted
Getting sleepy
Becoming confused
Giving less than 100%
Running out of time
Not concentrating
Making careless mistakes

Unit 5

Having a Master Plan

Covering Every Base

Taking tests had always been a nightmare for Andrew. During the first four years of elementary school, his grades were never above C and usually were Ds and even Fs. Not only were reading and math difficult for him, but he had another major problem: he got so nervous that he would often forget what he had studied.

By fifth grade, Andrew's skills had improved. The help he received from the resource teacher paid off, and he was now reading at grade level. His grades were better, too. In some of his classes, he was getting Bs, and he had even managed a B+ in science on his last report card. His math skills and writing skills had also improved, and he often received C+ or B- on math tests and book reports. Now that he was in ninth grade, the challenges were greater, but he continued to make progress. Tests still scared him, but Andrew realized that tests also scared the other kids who had never had learning problems and had never been in a resource program.

As he waited for the history test to be handed out, Andrew closed his eyes for about ten seconds and breathed deeply two or three times. In his mind, he saw himself knowing the answers to the questions, answering them confidently, and getting a good grade on the test. This helped calm him. He had studied hard for this history test, and he really wanted to do well.

Andrew had actually started preparing for the test a week ago. He had carefully reviewed his class notes, and he had re-read the chapter in the textbook. He had also kept to his study schedule. Although Andrew was nervous, he knew that he was well-prepared. He felt confident that he would get a decent grade if he could control his anxiety enough to concentrate.

Finally, the teacher handed out the test. Andrew quickly glanced at the questions and breathed a sigh of relief. He realized he would be able to answer all of the questions without difficulty. His study strategy had worked!

Putting the Plan into Action

Andrew created a study plan, and he carefully followed the plan as he studied for the test. What were the three steps in his strategy?

Step 1: rieviewd his notes

Step 2: reread chapter

Step 3: Kept his study schedeel

What three techniques did Andrew use to deal with his nervousness?

1. Closed his eyse
2. breathed deeply
3. imagined himself Passing the test

Can you think of any additional steps that Andrew might have taken to make certain he was prepared for the test? Write down ideas that were not mentioned in the story. (Hint: He could review the assignments that were recorded on his assignment sheet.). To help you find eight additional preparation steps, you may need to review quickly the studying techniques that have been covered in Units 1 – 4. Write down as many techniques as you can. You may even be able to find more than eight.

1. review his homework assignments
2. Quiz himself
3. make a pre-test
4. ___
5. ___
6. ___
7. ___
8. ___

Developing Your Own Master Study Plan

In Unit 4, you did an experiment in which you recorded your grades to see if they would improve if you eliminated or reduced distractions when you studied. It's time to do an experiment that incorporates **all** the studying procedures you have learned up to this point. For the next two weeks, do the following simple two-part experiment and see if it improves your school work. **REMEMBER:** *For this experiment to be effective, you must do it every day.*

Strategic-Studying Experiment

Part 1: **Make Sure You've Applied the Study-Skills Methods You Have Learned.**

Every day, check off each strategic-studying method you have used.

Effective-Studying Checklist

	YES	NO
• **I planned ahead.**	___	___
• **I followed my study schedule.**	___	___
• **I recorded my homework on my assignment sheet.**	___	___
• **I studied in a quiet place without distractions (telephone, TV, etc.).**	___	___
• **I studied sitting at a desk or a table.**	___	___
• **I had books and supplies needed to do my work.**	___	___
• **I organized my materials.**	___	___
• **I made sure my work was neat and legible.**	___	___
• **I carefully checked over my work to make sure I had eliminated mistakes.**	___	___
• **I submitted my completed assignments on time**	___	___
• **I kept track of my performance and my grades.**	___	___

Part 2: **KEEP TRACK OF YOUR PERFORMANCE** – Use all of the study procedures you have learned so far for two more weeks. Each day, record how you did on tests, homework assignments, and in-class assignments. In Unit 4, you learned how to reduce distractions, and you began keeping track of your performance using a different form. You may continue to use this form, or you can use the one on the next page which, as you can see, is designed differently. It would also be a

good idea to continue plotting your daily performance on a chart. Your teacher can give you additional copies of the forms and charts. (Punch holes in them and place them in a section in your binder called **Tracking Grades**)

If you are pleased with the results of this experiment, you may, of course, continue tracking your performance for as long as you want!

Keeping Track of My Performance

Day:__________ **Date:** ____________

Subject:	**Test Grades:**	**Reports:**	**Homework:**	**In-Class Work:**
____________	________	________	________	________
____________	________	________	________	________
____________	________	________	________	________
____________	________	________	________	________
____________	________	________	________	________

In the next unit, you will be taught methods for identifying, understanding, and remembering the important information you read in your textbooks. These methods will help you improve your grades and your academic self-confidence.

Part 2

Power-Charging Your Studying

Unit 6

Power-Reading

Comprehending and Remembering What You Read

Jeremy hated taking science tests for a very basic reason: studying meant that he would have to do a lot of reading. Since first grade, Jeremy had struggled with reading. To him, a "b" looked like a "d," and "*was*" looked like "*saw*." Understanding the information in his textbooks had always been equally challenging. He was so exhausted by sounding out the words that he didn't have enough energy left to figure out what the words actually meant. Although his reading was now much better than it had been before, he still dreaded having to study for a quiz or an exam.

Whenever Jeremy thought about the Friday's social-studies test, he became nervous. His stomach would begin to churn, and his hands would tremble. It was almost the end of the semester, and Jeremy realized that the test would probably determine whether he received a B- or a C+ in the course. He had worked very hard all semester long, and he had spent hours studying with his resource specialist and his mother at home. After all his hard work, he desperately wanted to get a B- in the course.

Jeremy's teacher had told the class that the test would cover the first section of a new science unit. As an experiment, she wanted to see how well the students could do without her having first covered the material in class. When Jeremy glanced at the assigned pages, he became very discouraged. There was so much complex information, and there were so many complicated facts to learn. Jeremy was certain he would never be able to understand and remember it all.

Just before he was about to sit down and start reading the unit, Jeremy's older sister came into his room and offered to show him a powerful study method. Kaitlin called the method "mind-mapping." She said that the method was also sometimes called "chunking." Because Kaitlin always got good grades, Jeremy was willing to listen to what she had to say. In fact, he was willing to try anything that could help him do better on the test.

As his sister began to describe the method to him, Jeremy quickly realized that mind-mapping could be fun. Kaitlin told him that he would be using pens and felt markers and that he would draw interesting designs and diagrams that connected the key ideas and facts.

Kaitlin told Jeremy that the first step was to look at the title of the unit and think about everything he already knew about the subject *before* actually reading the material. The second step was to turn the title into a question. She explained that he should do this *before* reading the material.

Jeremy looked at the title of the unit he was supposed to read. The title was "Lasers – Expanding the Frontiers of Science and Technology." He spent a few minutes reviewing all that he already knew about lasers. For example, he knew that doctors used lasers for surgery. He also knew that lasers could be used to cut through metal, and he knew that lasers could be used to aim guns.

Kaitlin told him that the third step in mind-mapping was to turn the title into a question. This was easy because his sister had given him a list of main-idea question words. The words were **HOW, WHY**, and **WHAT.** Jeremy chose the question word "HOW." At the top of the paper he wrote, *"How are lasers expanding the frontiers of science and technology?"* As Kaitlin instructed, he then put the piece of paper with the question to one side.

Kaitlin explained that the fourth step was to speed-read or skim the story, trying to pick out key ideas. She explained that when you speed-read, you do not actually read *every* word, you simply scan the material. She showed him how to use his fingers like a pointer, and she showed him how to force his eyes to skim the words looking for "clumps" of information. Kaitlin told him to skim the material and not worry about pronouncing each word in his mind. Because he had spent so much time in his resource program learning how to read words carefully and accurately, Jeremy found speed-reading very strange. Still, he was willing to try anything.

Speed-reading the three pages took less than three minutes. Kaitlin told him to try to remember as much as he could from this quick skimming. She also told him not to worry about the details and not to be concerned about what he couldn't remember. She reminded him that the purpose was to get an overview of the information in the unit.

It was now time to do step six and begin "mind-mapping." As Kaitlin instructed, Jeremy wrote the word "LASERS" in capital letters in the middle of a piece of unlined paper that he had turned horizontally. He chose a blue felt-tipped colored marker, and he drew a very creative box around it. Jeremy then read the material carefully and slowly and wrote down the key information on his paper. He used different-colored markers and connected the facts to the box in the middle of paper that said "LASERS." He drew boxes, circles, and ovals around each fact. He used straight lines, squiggly lines, curlicues, and arrows. As he read the material carefully and made diagrams to connect the information, Jeremy was amazed by how much he had learned about lasers.

When he finished adding information, Jeremy looked at his mind-map. Realizing that it looked a bit sloppy, he decided to recopy the map and make it look neater. Once he was finished doing so, he studied the diagrams he had drawn. He was very proud and very surprised. He had not realized that he was such a good artist!

Jeremy was ready for the final step. He reached for the paper on which he had written the question *"How are lasers expanding the frontiers of science and technology*?" Jeremy usually hated writing essays, but this one was easy. He used his mind-map to answer the questions, and he was careful to include all the important information he had written on his map. He then edited the essay and corrected some spelling and grammar mistakes. When he reread his one-page essay, he was very impressed with his own work.

Before the test on Friday, Jeremy planned to read the unit again very carefully. He also planned on carefully reviewing the information in his mind-map on Thursday night. The final step in preparing for the test would involve re-reading his essay answer to the main-idea question.

When the teacher handed back Jeremy's test, Jeremy discovered that he did not get the B- he had so desperately wanted. He got a B! On the top of the paper, his teacher had written "Congratulations!" Jeremy couldn't wait to show the test to his parents. One thing was certain. He planned on using mind-mapping again.

Learning a Method for Studying More Effectively

You are now going to read the same science unit that Jeremy read and practice the steps of the mind-mapping procedure. As you already know, the title of the unit is "Lasers: A New Frontier in Technology."

Step 1: Turn the title into a **main-idea question.** Use main idea question words: **HOW, WHY, WHAT**. (This should be easy. In the story, Jeremy showed you this step.)

Question: ____

____?

Step 2: Write down what you know about lasers. You probably already know some information about lasers. You've seen them in movies and on TV. You've seen them used in supermarkets to scan the barcodes on groceries. Write down all you can remember *before* you read the unit.

What I Already Know about Lasers

1. ____
2. ____
3. ____
4. ____
5. ____
6. ____
7. ____

Learning How to Speed-Read

It's time to speed-read. Look at the diagram below. Notice how the fingers form a "pointer" that allows you to scan the words easily, without reading or pronouncing each word in your mind.

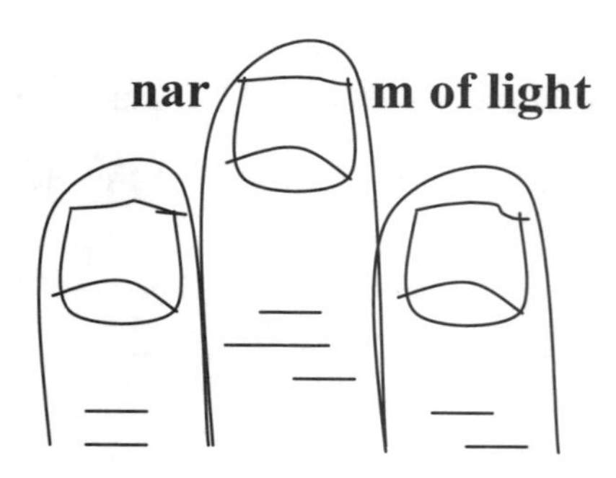

Move your fingers quickly across each line from left to right. Force your eyes to "scan" or skim. **Don't try to read each word carefully**. Although you have been taught to read words very carefully in school, speed-reading is a different type of skill. In some situations, you will still need to read material carefully. For example, you always want to read the instructions for a test very accurately. Speed-reading is a method that can be very helpful when you first begin to study something new. It helps you get an "overview" of the material.

Practice speed-reading the unit. Spend no more than ***three minutes*** scanning the material. Do not expect to remember a great deal of information. You just want to know the content. Forcing yourself to scan material quickly will probably be challenging at first because you are not used to this technique. With practice, however, the method will become easy!

LASERS

Expanding the Frontiers of Science and Technology

Imagine a very narrow beam of light capable of drilling two hundred holes on a spot as tiny as the head of a pin and powerful enough to pierce a diamond, the hardest natural substance. This intense beam of light can be also be used to trigger a small nuclear reaction or to reach the moon more than 250,000 miles away.

In 1960, an American scientist named Theodore H. Maiman built a machine that could produce this light. He called his invention a laser. The word is an *acronym* whose letters stand for Light Amplification by Stimulated Emission of Radiation.

Types of Lasers

Today there are four main types of lasers: solid-state, semiconductor, gas-discharge, and dye lasers. These devices can range in size from as small as a grain of salt to as large as a football field.

Transforming Energy into Intense Light

Lasers typically have three main parts: an *energy source*, a substance called an *active medium* (also called a *resonator*), and a structure enclosing the active medium known as an *optical cavity*. The energy source typically supplies an electric current. The flash of energy is absorbed by the active medium. The atoms in the active medium--usually a gas or synthetic material--are excited, and the energy level increases. This energy is temporarily stored and then discharged in the form of light waves. Mirrors at the ends of the optical cavity reflect the light back into the active medium. More atoms are excited, and additional energy is produced. The light grows increasingly intense. The energy exits the laser as a narrow beam that may be visible, or invisible when the beam is comprised exclusively of radiation.

Distinguishing Ordinary Light from Laser Light

The light discharged by the excited particles in a laser differs from the light produced by a light bulb or fluorescent lamp. In the case of a florescent lamp, a current of electricity excites the electrons in the mercury vapor inside the tube. The waves of light shoot out in all directions and do not reach very far. This explains why there may be dark shadows in the corners of a large room even though the lights are turned on.

Ordinary light travels like ocean waves during a storm. The distance from the top of one wave to the next is called a *wavelength.* Because the different wavelengths tumble over each other and travel in many directions at once, the total amount of produced energy is low.

Unlike ordinary light, the beam produced by a laser consists of a single wavelength. The waves move in the same direction like an arrow. The result is a strong, straight ray that has remarkable power.

A laser beam does not spread out over long distances. A beam aimed at the moon might light up a spot only two or three miles wide. Although an ordinary beam of light from a searchlight could not possibly reach the moon, if it could, the lighted area would spread out more than 25,000 miles!

Because a laser beam is a *single* wave length, it can focus intense light and heat on a very small area. A laser beam can actually generate heat three times as hot as the temperature of the sun which is 32,000 degrees Fahrenheit!

Using Lasers

Lasers can be found in homes, factories, stores, offices, hospitals, and libraries. The intense light has many applications that include welding tiny intricate electronic circuits, storing computer data, and reading the prices recorded on the bar code for items in a store. Lasers can also be used to record music, make movies, and produce three-dimensional images called holograms. These holograms are imprinted on credit cards and on advertising displays, artwork, and jewelry.

Surgeons use lasers to perform delicate operations such as welding a detached retina back to the eyeball. A laser can also be used as a scalpel to remove tumors, scars, or even tattoos. Because the intense heat stops the flow of blood, there is very little bleeding during surgery.

Lasers are also useful in measuring distances. By pointing the beam at a target, technicians can measure the exact time required for the light beam to bounce back. In contrast, radar bounces an electronic pulse off an object and measures how long it takes for the pulse to bounce back. Because light-beam measurement can indicate the target's location and distance with great accuracy, scientists regularly use lasers to track satellites that are specially equipped with light-reflecting mirrors.

The straight-line beam of the laser also has many military applications. A weapon with a laser sight can aim a beam of light on a target. Because the beam shows precisely where the bullet, missile, or bomb will hit, weapons equipped with lasers are highly accurate and reliable.

Fiber-optics communication is another field where lasers have great value. The electrical signals of telephone calls and televisions pictures are transformed into pulses or burst of laser light. Thin strands of glass called optical fibers conduct the light. These strands are no thicker than a human hair. All the energy is passed through the fiber, and one fiber can carry as much information as several thousand copper telephone wires. A single beam could actually transmit all the information in an encyclopedia in a fraction of a second!

Today, lasers are essential tools in virtually every area. In the years ahead, new and even more remarkable uses will undoubtedly be discovered. These applications will continually expand the frontiers of science and technology.

Practicing Mind-Mapping

You are ready to learn the next step of the mind-mapping method. What have you learned from skimming the material that you didn't know before? Write down any new information you have learned from skimming the material.

What I Have Learned about Lasers from Speed-Reading

1. ______________________________
2. ______________________________
3. ______________________________
4. ______________________________
5. ______________________________

Step 3: Mind-map the material. It's time to become an artist! You will need colored pencils or felt tip pens. Use one of your pens or pencils to write the word "Lasers" in the center of a piece of unlined paper. (You can use a different color for each letter in the word if you want.) Draw boxes or circles around the key information. Connect the boxes or circle to the word *laser*. You can also connect chunks of information to other chunks of related information with lines or arrows. Be as creative as you like in making designs around the information you put down. Use colors that you like. Remember to write small so that you can fit all the key information on a piece of paper. Put only key ideas in your mind-map and leave out unnecessary words. If you can't fit everything on one page, tape two pieces of paper together. Plan ahead so that you have enough room to draw the boxes and arrows. Draw lines to show how the information in the unit is linked to the main ideas. Have fun! If you are having difficulty getting started, use the following sample mind-map as a guide.

Sample Mind-Map

You might find it interesting to compare what you have included in your mind-map with the sample below. This is only a partial mind-map to help you get started.

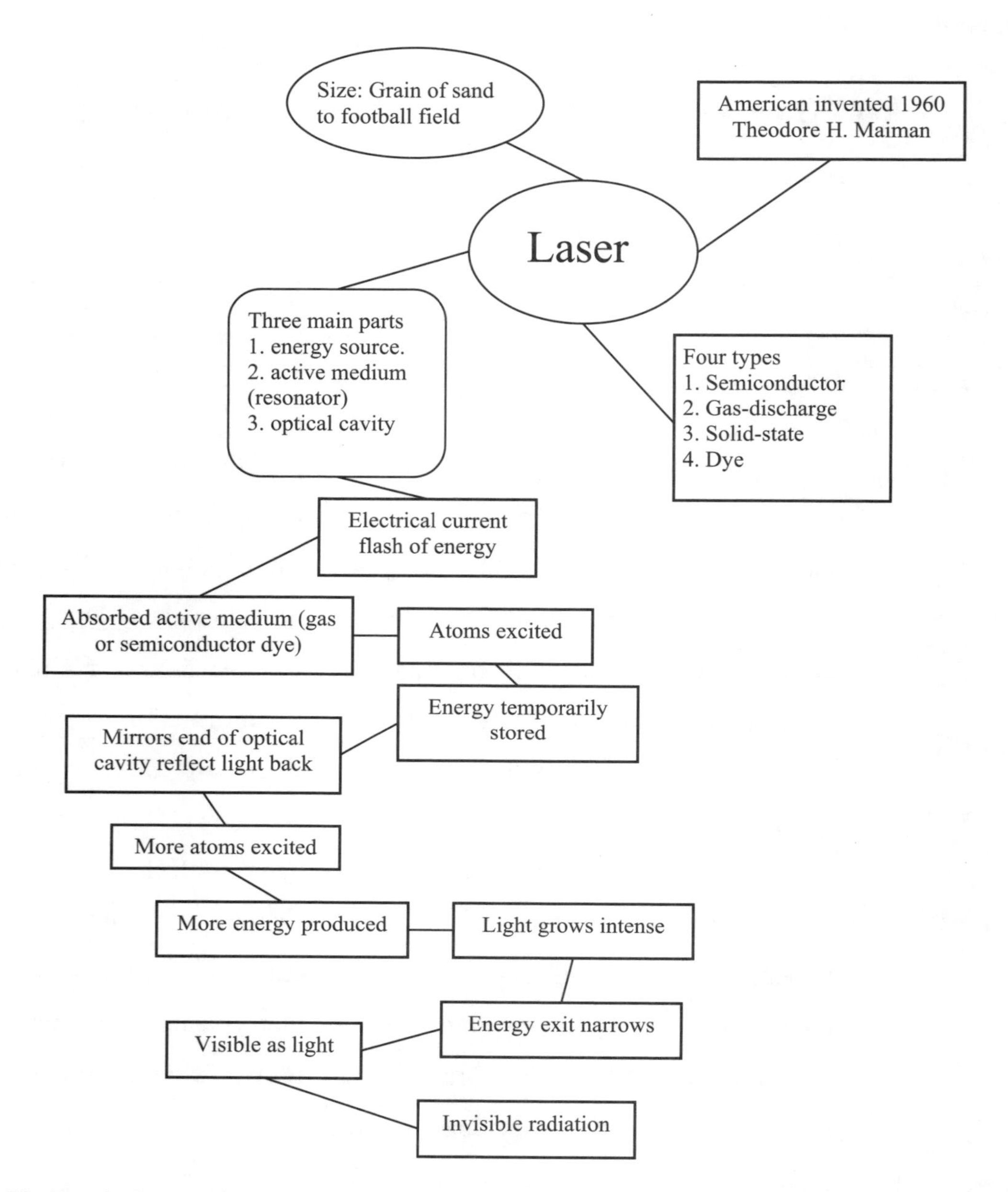

Your mind-map does not have to look exactly like the partial sample. The sample is here for comparison and to give you ideas about what information to add to your own mind-map.

When you have completed your mind-map, compare it to the completed sample on the following page. The sample may include certain information that you omitted, and it may omit information that you included. If you think there is information you should have included, expand your mind-map. If your mind-map is sloppy or hard-to-read, take the time to redo it.

Completed Mind-Map

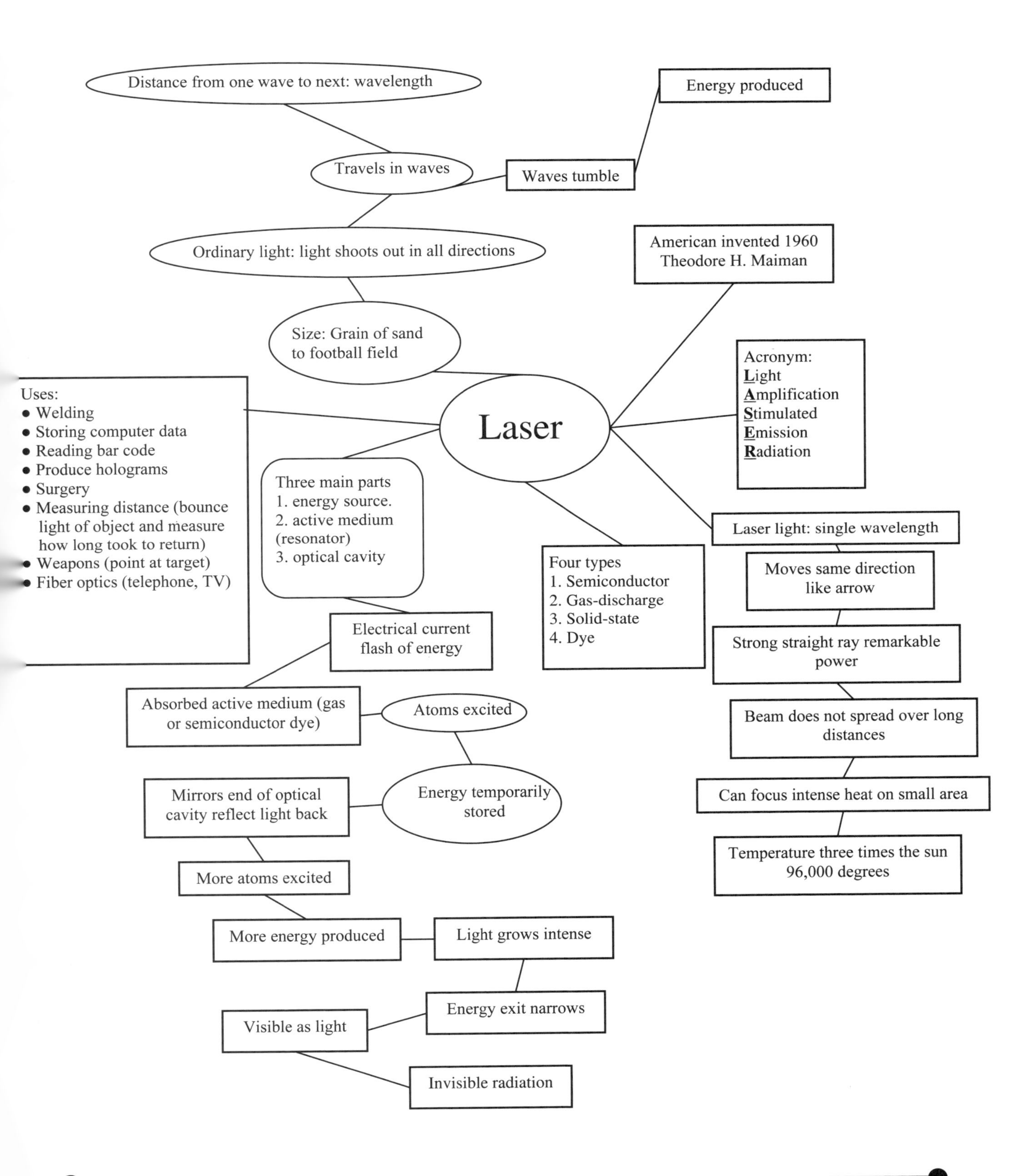

Some students like to draw mind-maps that are very creative and artistic. The key is to become actively involved in the process. If drawing an artistic mind-map helps you do so and helps you understand and remember the information, that's great!

Sample Artistic Mind-Map

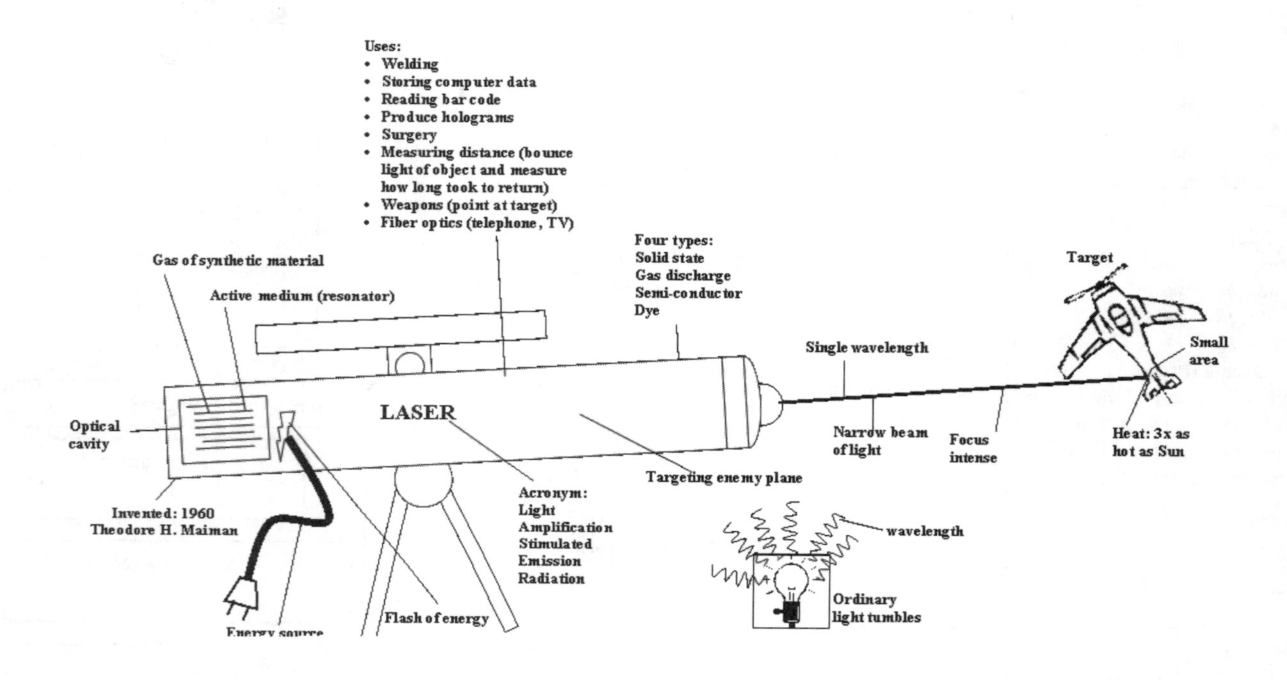

Reviewing and Completing the Mind-Mapping Steps

Step 1: **Write down everything you know about the subject before reading the material.**

Step 2: **Turn the title into a main-idea question.**

Step 3: **Speed-read the material.**

Step 4: **Read the material carefully and slowly, and mind-map.**

Step 5: **Recopy your mind-map if it is sloppy or illegible.**

It's now time to do Step 6.

Step 6: **Answer the title question.**

Use your mind-map to help you locate information and write a paragraph that answers the main idea question you wrote down before reading the unit: *"How are lasers expanding the frontiers of science and technology?"* Remember to use a powerful topic sentence (beginning sentence). If you wish, you can use the following sample topic sentence to begin your essay. If you prefer, make up your own topic sentence. Once you choose your topic sentence, complete your answer to the question by including the key information in your mind-map that tells how the laser has contributed to modern technology.

Sample Topic Sentence:

In 1960, an American scientist named Theodore H. Maiman invented the laser, and this invention has changed modern technology.

How Are Lasers Expanding the Frontiers of Science and Technology?

____

____

____

____

____

____

Carefully proofread your essay to find spelling and grammar mistakes. If your essay is sloppy, recopy it on another piece of paper.

What I Have Learned about Mind-Mapping

The following mind-mapping steps are out of the order. Number each step in the correct order.

Step __: **Answer the title question**.

Step __: **Write down everything you know about the subject before reading the material.**

Step __: **Turn the title into a main-idea question.**

Step __: **Recopy your mind-map if it is sloppy or illegible.**

Step __: **Read the material carefully and slowly, and do your mind-map.**

Step __: **Speed-read the material.**

Look back to page 81 and see if you numbered the steps properly.

Unit 7

Powering Up Your Reading Comprehension

Confronting a Disaster

Wyatt desperately wanted to get a B on the history final. After having studied harder than he had ever studied before, he was convinced that he knew the material backwards and forwards. During the preceding week, he had spent more than three hours with his resource specialist, going over the six units that would be covered by the test, and he had spent more than four additional hours studying at home. He had re-read the unit, and he had carefully reviewed his class notes. He was certain that he had done everything possible to prepare.

As he waited for his teacher to hand out the test, Wyatt felt very confident. "With all of the studying I've done, I have to get a good grade." he thought. Wyatt imagined showing his test with a big B written at the top to his parents, and he imagined how proud they would be.

Finally, the test was passed to him. As he scanned the questions, Wyatt felt fear surge through his body. It was as if he were looking at a test covering material that he had never seen before! His fear quickly turned to panic, and his mind began to shut down. "I'm going to fail!" a voice inside his head screamed. As he began to write, Wyatt thought that he would only be able to answer ten out of the twenty questions. The more upset he became, the more he forgot, and the more he forgot, the more upset he became.

When he finally handed in the test, Wyatt felt sick in the pit of his stomach. He felt that he would be lucky to get a D. He now dreaded having to show the test to his parents.

Weighing the Options

No one can accuse Wyatt of being unmotivated or irresponsible. He had a goal, and he did everything he could think of to prepare for the test. He had spent hours studying. Having worked so hard, he felt justifiably confident that he would do well on the test. But then something terrible and unexpected happened. He couldn't remember information that his history teacher obviously wanted the class to know. What could have gone wrong? Did he study the wrong material? Had he not understood what he had studied? Did he have difficulty recalling key information? Did he panic? Did he expect a different kind of test than the one the teacher gave?

You may have had a similar "nightmare." At one time or another, every student experiences a major disappointment in school. Everyone makes miscalculations, and everyone must deal with the consequences of these miscalculations. You may do the wrong math problems for homework or forget to include important facts in a book report. The result is a lowered grade. If you think smart, you will analyze the setback, learn from your mistake, and do everything in your power to avoid making the same error again. Instead of giving up, you will figure out a plan for doing better the next time. This persistence, determination, and strategic thinking are often described as "having grit," "having character," and "thinking smart."

Wyatt was at a crossroads. He had three options, and each option had predictable consequences.

Option #1: He could give up and accept that he will do poorly on tests no matter how hard he tries.

Probable Consequences: Frustration, loss of confidence, loss of pride, and poor grades.

Option #2: He could continue to use the same study strategy.

Probable Consequences: Frustration, loss of confidence, loss of pride, and poor grades.

Option #3: He could analyze his miscalculation, identify the reason for his poor performance, and make adjustments in his study strategy.

Probable Consequences: Improved grades, more confidence, more pride.

Let's say that Wyatt selects option #3. He analyzes what happened and concludes that he did not really understand what he was studying, and he did not recall important information. He decides that he needs to learn a more effective way to prepare for tests, and he asks his teacher for help. She suggests that he learn a powerful study system called the "Chewing-Up Information" Method.

You are now going to learn this powerful study system. Before doing so, you need to understand what actually goes on in your brain when you read and study.

How the Brain Works When You Read

When you were reading about lasers in Unit 6, your brain was absorbing important information through your eyes. This information was communicated in the form of words. As you read, the words were beamed like a TV picture from the page to your brain. Your brain then connected the words with their meaning. For example, when you read the word "mirror," you immediately linked the word with its meaning. You were able to do so because you are familiar with the word. Without even realizing it, you may have formed a mental picture of a mirror as you read the word.

In the unit, you also read the word "acronym." You may or may not have seen this word before. Although acronym was defined in the story, you probably had to think about the word more carefully than you did the word "mirror." To help you remember what the acronym LASER means, you would most likely have to recite it several times and link the five words that make up the acronym. As you learned what the word stood for, you may have said to yourself, "I never knew that!" Or perhaps you thought, "Hey, that's cool how they made up this word."

In many ways, your brain works like a very fast and powerful computer. It absorbs information, "digests" it, recalls it, and then tells you what to do with it. Your brain usually works very quickly. For example, if you were asked "Who was the first President of the United States?" or "How much is 9 + 2?," you would probably be able to answer these questions in an instant.

You have already learned a powerful method named mind-mapping that can help you understand and remember information when you study. You are now going to learn another way to control your brain's on-board computer. The technique is called the "Chewing-Up Information" Method. To learn this new method, we are going to use the material about lasers that you read and mind-mapped in Unit 6.

You may be thinking, "Why learn another study method? I like mind-mapping!" The answer is simple. By learning different techniques for reading and studying effectively, you can choose the one that works best for you. You may even discover that you like the new method you are about to learn more than mind-mapping. You may decide that in some study situations you prefer to use mind-mapping and in other study situations you prefer use the "Chewing-Up Information" Method because it helps you take apart, "digest," and remember key ideas and facts. You may even decide to combine parts of both methods and create your own personalized study system.

The "Chewing-Up Information" Method

STEP 1: **Turn the title into a question before you read the material.** (You have already learned this step in Unit 6!)

Reason: Asking a question about what you are about to read before you actually start to read encourages you to *think about* what you are reading and helps you better *understand* the content.

Title: *"Lasers – Expanding the Frontiers of Science and Technology"*

Question: How are lasers expanding the frontiers of science and technology?

Answer: Because you are asking this question *before* you read the material, you do not yet have enough information to answer the question. (Let's assume that you are seeing this material for the first time and that you haven't mind-mapped it.) **Do not attempt to answer the question. Let your mind simply think about it as you read the material.**

How to Use Question Words

Example of a Main-Idea Question:	**How** are lasers expanding the frontiers of science and technology?
Example of a Detail Question:	**When** were lasers invented?
Question Words:	**How, When, Where, Why, What, Which, Who**
Main-Idea Question Words:	**How, Why, What** **Why** did the American colonies declare independence from England?
Detail Question Words:	**When, Where, Which, Who** **Where** is the Grand Canyon?

Use one of the Main-Idea Question Words to change the following titles into questions.

Title: "Discovering a New Medical Breakthrough"
Question: How was the new medical breakthrough discovered?

Title: "Methods for Improving Farming"
Question: ____?

Title: "Using Computers in Medical Research"
Question: ____?

Title: "Killer Bees"
Question: ____?

Title: "Controlling Illegal Drugs"
Question: ____?

Title: "Winning the War of Independence"
Question: ____?

Now figure out the title from the following main-idea question.

Question: How did Cleopatra become Queen of Egypt?

Title: Cleopatra--The Queen of Egypt

Question: Why did America declare war against Japan?

Title: ____________________

Question: What are the three branches of the United States government?

Title: ____________________

Question: How are crops protected from hungry insects?

Title: ____________________

Question: Why do sharks attack?

Title: ____________________

Question: How can weather patterns be studied?

Title: ____________________

Question: How do you study effectively?

Title: ____________________

Learning More Steps in the "Chewing-Up Information" Method

In Step 1 you turned the main title into a question. In Step 2, you do the same with subtitles.

STEP 2: Turn each subtitle into a question before reading the section.

Reason: You do this step for the same reason you do Step 1. Posing questions about the content in each section of a unit before you read the material helps you focus and think about the information when you do begin to read. Depending on the information, you may decide to ask either a Main-Idea Question or a Detail Question.

Subtitle 1: Types of Lasers

Question: What are the types of lasers?

Do not attempt to answer this question yet. Let your mind think about it as you read the section.

Now go through the unit. Write down each subtitle, and then turn each subtitle into a Main-Idea Question.

Subtitle 2: Transforming Energy into Intense Light

Question 2: How is energy transformed into intense light?

Subtitle 3: ____

Question 3: ____

Subtitle 4: ____

Question 4: ____

STEP 3: **Speed-read the material one time.** If you need to review the instructions for speed-reading, turn to page 74.

STEP 4: **Re-read the material carefully, using a highlighter or pencil to underline key ideas in each paragraph**.

Important: You are permitted to highlight and/or underline in this workbook. However, when you use the "CHEWING-UP INFORMATION" METHOD with school textbooks, do not underline or highlight in them! Other students will be using these books next year. Marking your books would not be fair to them. Later, you will learn how to take notes without having to highlight or underline. You will record the important information directly onto binder paper.

Let's look at how the first four paragraphs might look when you do Step 4 and underline or highlight key ideas.

LASERS

Expanding the Frontiers of Science and Technology

Imagine a very narrow beam of light capable of drilling two hundred holes on a spot as tiny as the head of a pin and powerful enough to pierce a diamond, the hardest natural substance. This intense beam of light can be also be used to trigger a small nuclear reaction or to reach the moon more than 250,000 miles away.

In 1960, an American scientist named Theodore H. Maiman built a machine that could produce this intense light. He called his invention a laser. The word is an *acronym* whose letters stand for Light Amplification by Stimulated Emission of Radiation.

Types of Lasers

Today there are four main types of lasers: solid-state, semiconductor, gas-discharge, and dye lasers. These devices can range in size from as small as a grain of salt to as large as a football field.

Transforming Energy into Intense Light

Lasers typically have three main parts: an *energy source*, a substance called an *active medium* (also called a *resonator*), and a structure enclosing the active medium known as an *optical cavity*. The energy source typically supplies an electric current. The flash of energy is absorbed by the active medium. The atoms in the active medium--usually a gas or synthetic material--are excited, and the energy level increases. This energy is temporarily stored and then discharged in the form of light waves. Mirrors at the ends of the optical cavity reflect the light back into the active medium. More atoms are excited, and additional energy is produced. The light grows increasingly intense. The energy exits the laser as a narrow beam that may be visible, or invisible when the beam is comprised of exclusively of radiation.

Underlining or Highlighting on Your Own

The entire laser unit is printed on the next page. Underline or highlight the first four paragraphs just as they appear above. Then re-read the rest of the unit and continue to underline or highlight the **KEY INFORMATION** on your own. Remember to leave out words like "the," "a," "their," and "of." Highlight only the most important words.

LASERS

Expanding the Frontiers of Science and Technology

Imagine a very narrow beam of light capable of drilling two hundred holes on a spot as tiny as the head of a pin and powerful enough to pierce a diamond, the hardest natural substance. This intense beam of light can be also be used to trigger a small nuclear reaction or to reach the moon more than 250,000 miles away.

In 1960, an American scientist named Theodore H. Maiman built a machine that could produce this light. He called his invention a laser. The word is an *acronym* whose letters stand for Light Amplification by Stimulated Emission of Radiation.

Types of Lasers

Today there are four main types of lasers: solid-state, semiconductor, gas-discharge, and dye lasers. These devices can range in size from as small as a grain of salt to as large as a football field.

Transforming Energy into Intense Light

Lasers typically have three main parts: an *energy source*, a substance called an *active medium* (also called a *resonator*), and a structure enclosing the active medium known as an *optical cavity*. The energy source typically supplies an electric current. The flash of energy is absorbed by the active medium. The atoms in the active medium--usually a gas or synthetic material--are excited, and the energy level increases. This energy is temporarily stored and then discharged in the form of light waves. Mirrors at the ends of the optical cavity reflect the light back into the active medium. More atoms are excited, and additional energy is produced. The light grows increasingly intense. The energy exits the laser as a narrow beam that may be visible, or invisible when the beam is comprised exclusively of radiation.

Distinguishing Ordinary Light from Laser Light

The light discharged by the excited particles in a laser differs from the light produced by a light bulb or fluorescent lamp. In the case of a florescent lamp, a current of electricity excites the electrons in the mercury vapor inside the tube. The waves of light shoot out in all directions and do not reach very far. This explains why there may be dark shadows in the corners of a large room even though the lights are turned on.

Ordinary light travels like ocean waves during a storm. The distance from the top of one wave to the next is called a *wavelength.* Because the different wavelengths tumble over each other and travel in many directions at once, the total amount of produced energy is low.

Unlike ordinary light, the beam produced by a laser consists of a single wavelength. The waves move in the same direction like an arrow. The result is a strong, straight ray that has remarkable power.

A laser beam does not spread out over long distances. A beam aimed at the moon might light up a spot only two or three miles wide. Although an ordinary beam of light from a searchlight could not possibly reach the moon, if it could, the lighted area would spread out more than 25,000 miles!

Because a laser beam is a *single* wavelength, it can focus intense light and heat on a very small area. A laser beam can actually generate heat three times as hot as the temperature of the sun which is 32,000 degrees Fahrenheit!

Using Lasers

Lasers can be found in homes, factories, stores, offices, hospitals, and libraries. The intense light has many applications that include welding tiny intricate electronic circuits, storing computer data, and reading the prices recorded on the bar code for items in a store. Lasers can also be used to record music, make movies, and produce three-dimensional images called holograms. These holograms are imprinted on credit cards and on advertising displays, artwork, and jewelry.

Surgeons use lasers to perform delicate operations such as welding a detached retina back to the eyeball. A laser can also be used as a scalpel to remove tumors, scars, or even tattoos. Because the intense heat stops the flow of blood, there is very little bleeding during surgery.

Lasers are also useful in measuring distances. By pointing the beam at a target, technicians can measure the exact time required for the beam to bounce back. In contrast, radar bounces an electronic pulse off an object and measures how long it takes for the pulse to bounce back. Because light beam measurement can indicate the target's location and distance with great accuracy, scientists regularly use lasers to track satellites that are specially equipped with light-reflecting mirrors.

The straight-line beam of the laser also has many military applications. A weapon with a laser sight can aim a beam of light on a target. Because the beam shows precisely where the bullet, missile, or bomb will hit, weapons equipped with lasers are highly accurate and reliable.

Fiber-optics communication is another field where lasers have great value. The electrical signals of telephone calls and television pictures are transformed into pulses or bursts of laser light. Thin strands of glass called optical fibers conduct the light. These strands are no thicker than a human hair. All the energy is passed through the fiber, and one fiber can carry as much information as several thousand copper telephone wires. A single beam could actually transmit all the information in an encyclopedia in a fraction of a second!

Today, lasers are essential tools in virtually every area. In the years ahead, new and even more remarkable uses will undoubtedly be discovered. These applications will continually expand the frontiers of science and technology.

Answering the Subtitle Questions and the Title Question

It is now time to answer the subtitle questions you posed in **Step 2** of the "Chewing-Up Information" Method. Then answer the title question. Use a complete sentence. As you can see, the first two questions are answered for you. Answer the subtitle questions #3 and #4 on your own. You can refer back to the information you highlighted while writing your answer.

STEP 5: **Answer Subtitle Questions.**

Subtitle Question 1: *What are the types of lasers?*
Sample Answer: Lasers range in size from as small as a grain of sand to as large as a football field. There are four main types of lasers: solid-state, semiconductor, gas-discharge, and dye lasers.

Subtitle Question 2: *How is energy transformed into intense light?*
Sample Answer: A flash of energy excites the atoms in the active medium located in the optical cavity. The energy level increases. The energy is temporarily stored and then discharged as light waves. Mirrors at the ends of the optical cavity reflect the light back into the active medium where more atoms are exited. The light grows more intense and is released as a narrow visible or invisible beam.

Subtitle Question 3: *What are the types of lasers?*

Your Answer: ____

____

____

Subtitle Question 4: *What are the uses of lasers? (or "How are lasers used?")*

Your Answer: ____

____

____

____

STEP 6: **Answer the Title Question**

Title question: *How Are Lasers Expanding the Frontiers of Science and Technology?*

[You have already answered this title question after you mind-mapped the laser section in Unit 6. You do not need to rewrite the essay, unless your teacher asks you to. Your teacher may want you to expand your original essay now that you have underlined or highlighted key information and identified additional details and facts. Your teacher may also want you to practice your writing skills. If you are asked to rewrite the essay, use a separate sheet of notebook paper.]

A Practice Quiz

By now, you know a great deal about lasers! It's time to take a quiz to see how much you have learned using the "Chewing-Up Information" Method. Put away your mind-map and don't look at the information you highlighted in the laser unit.

1. Lasers can be of the following types:
   - A. a solid-state device.
   - B. a gas-discharge device
   - C. a semiconductor device
   - D. a dye device
   - E. all of the above

2. Lasers can be used to determine the location of a target by bouncing an electronic pulse off the target.

   A. True

   B. False

3. Lasers discharge excess energy when the atoms in the active medium are excited and the energy level increases

   A. True

   B. False

4. Mirrors in the optical cavity point the light beam from the laser to the outside.

   A. True

   B. False

5. The light produced by a laser beam is hot because the rays tumble.

   A. True

   B. False

6. Light waves from a fluorescent lamp and a laser are alike because they

   A. require an energy source.

   B. made up of different wavelengths.

   C. controlled in their direction of movement.

7. If a laser beam from the earth reached the moon, the area that would be lighted would be

   A. one mile wide

   B. 25,000 miles wide

   C. two or three miles wide

8. A laser can get

   A. as hot as the sun (10,600 degrees Fahrenheit)

   B. twice as hot as the sun (21,200 degrees Fahrenheit)

   C. three times as hot as the sun (32,000 degrees Fahrenheit)

9. A satellite that can be located by a laser must be

   A. equipped with light-reflecting mirrors

   B. transmitting electronic pulses

   C. orbiting less than 500 miles away

10. Lasers were invented in 1964.
    A. True
    B. False
11. Lasers are produced by the collision of several wavelengths.
    A. True
    B. False
12. The acronym laser stands for: ________ ________ ________ ________ ________
13. List five uses of lasers: ________________________, ________________________

________________________, ________________________, ________________________

Examining How You Did on the Quiz

Possibility #1: You did very well on the test. (No more than **1** incorrect answer.)

Possibility #2: You did well on the test. (**2** wrong answers.)

Possibility #3: You had difficulty with the test. (**3** or more incorrect answers.)

If you had several incorrect answers, look back at what you highlighted. Did you highlight the information that was asked on the test? Did you have difficulty remembering the information?

If you had trouble with the test, don't worry. In Unit 8 you will learn additional methods for preparing for tests. But before you work on improving your test-taking skills, you have to learn how to take good notes.

In the next unit, you'll learn how to take "standard notes." You'll also practice answering title and subtitle questions. Because you've already highlighted or underlined the unit, *you've done most of the work involved in taking notes.* You'll discover that note-taking is easy!

Answers: 1. E 2. True 3. True 4. False 5. False 6. A 7. C 8. C 9. A 10. F 11. F

12. Light Amplification by Stimulated Emission of Radiation
13. **Possible uses include:** recording music reading bar codes storing computer disks making movies surgery making holograms measuring distance tracking satellites aiming weapons welding circuits telephone or TV fiber optics

What I Have Learned about Reading Comprehension

Number in the proper order the six steps in the **"Chewing-Up Information" Method.**

Step __ = Turn each subtitle into a question using either a main-idea question word or a detail question word.

Step __ = Re-read material carefully and highlight or underline key information.

Step __ = Turn the title into a question using a main-idea question word.

Step __ = Answer the title question.

Step __ = Answer the subtitle questions.

Step __ = Speed-read the material.

The **Main-Idea Questions** are: ____________ ____________ ____________

The **Detail Questions** are: ____________ ____________ ____________ ____________

True/False

The "Chewing-Up Information" Method requires some extra time.	**T**	**F**
You should use a highlighter in your school textbooks.	**T**	**F**
As long as you memorize the important information, you don't need to understand it.	**T**	**F**
Asking title and subtitle questions before you read helps you think about the content.	**T**	**F**
You should answer the questions about the title and subtitles before reading the material.	**T**	**F**
If have a problem, you usually need to analyze it carefully before you can solve it.	**T**	**F**
Figuring out what went wrong helps reduce the chances of repeating the same mistake.	**T**	**F**
Reading material one or two times is enough when studying for a test.	**T**	**F**
You should only underline or highlight the most important information, and you should leave out all words that are not important.	**T**	**F**
Answering the subtitle questions will help you have a better overall understanding of the material you are studying.	**T**	**F**
Answering the title question will help you have a more complete understanding of the material.	**T**	**F**

Unit 8

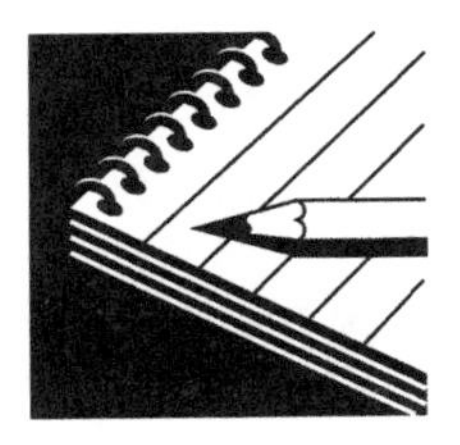

Taking Notes

Preparing for a Test

Carlos was certain that he wanted to be a Navy pilot. He loved flying, and the idea of piloting a fighter jet and landing it on an aircraft carrier enthralled him. He had already taken six plane trips with his parents. Buckling his seat belt and being pressed into the back of his seat during the steep takeoffs were incredibly exciting. On one trip, he remembered looking down on the enormous blanket of white "cotton-puff" clouds that covered the earth. This had been an unbelievable experience. Carlos had already decided that he would become a commercial pilot when he retired from the Navy. He could then fly all over the world.

Carlos realized, of course, that to become a Navy pilot he would have to go to college. He was determined to get good grades, but there was a complication. He had learning problems. Although his math was excellent, reading had always been difficult for him. After four years in the resource program, he was finally reading at grade level. He was glad his resource specialist was now focusing on improving his study skills. He knew that if he was going to be accepted into a four-year college, he would need to learn some powerful methods for improving his comprehension and his test grades.

Carlos' immediate goal was to get at least a B on Friday's science test. If he did, he would have a good chance of getting a B in the course.

When he arrived home from school on Monday, Carlos wrote down his study plan:

Monday:
1. Speed-read the unit about Egypt.
2. Make up main-idea essay questions from the title and subtitles.
3. Read the unit carefully.
4. Draw mind-map.

Tuesday:
1. Re-read the unit.
2. Expand the mind-map.

Wednesday:
1. Take notes in "standard form."
2. Answer questions from title and subtitles.

Thursday:
1. Write key facts on index cards.
2. Make up practice test detail questions from notes.
3. Review notes, mind-map, and index cards.

Carlos estimated he would have to study approximately two hours and thirty minutes to prepare for the history test. He calculated that he would need to study for approximately forty minutes each evening, Monday through Thursday. If he disciplined himself, he was confident that he could make his study plan work. For Carlos, spending two hours and thirty minutes was a small price to pay for a good grade on the test. The payoff would make the hard work worthwhile.

Learning How to Take Notes

You have already learned several powerful techniques for studying more effectively. You know how to *establish a study schedule, manage time, control distractions when you study, record assignments accurately,* and *ask and answer questions* as you read. You know how to *identify important information.* You also know how to *organize* this information into a *mind-map* so that you can understand and remember the important ideas and details.

In Unit 7, you learned another powerful studying procedure called the **"Chewing-Up Information" Method.** As you recall, the last step in the system was to identify and highlight or underline the important information. You also learned how to distinguish between main ideas and details. You were told that the highlighting or underlining was for practice only because you are not permitted to mark up your textbooks.

You are now going to learn another way to organize and record information. The method is called "Standard Note-Taking." The steps are the same as in "Chewing-Up Information," but instead of highlighting or underlining the important information **(Step 4)**, you are going to transfer this information directly from the unit into notes without marking up your textbook.

Let's first review the "Chewing-Up Information" steps. *Note that Step 4 has been changed.* After reading the material carefully, you are to take notes instead of highlighting or underlining.

"Chewing-Up Information" Steps

STEP 1: **Turn the title into a question before reading the material.** (The main-idea question words are: *How, Why,* and *What*). Write the question on the top line of a piece of binder paper. Begin writing at the left margin.

STEP 2: **Turn each subtitle into a question before reading the material.** Depending on the content, choose either a main-idea or detail question word. Indent below the subtitle question and leave space to write notes under each question. Use a pencil in case you have to erase.

STEP 3: **Speed-read the material.**

STEP 4: **Read the material carefully. As you read, write down key information in note form.** (See sample of "Standard Note-Taking" on page 106.)

You're now going to put the key information into standard note-taking form. Remember:

- **Write down only important information.**
- **Leave out unnecessary words.**
- **Abbreviate whenever possible.**
- **Write neatly and legibly.**
- **Indent your notes under each question.**

When taking notes under each subtitle question, do not try to answer the question in your notes. Simply write down all the important information that deals with the subject. As you have already highlighted or underlined this information in Unit 7, this should be a "piece of cake." Later, after you have finished taking notes, you'll use your notes to answer each subtitle question.

Using Abbreviations

You can save time by using abbreviations when you take notes, but you must be able to understand your own abbreviations! In Unit 2, you were provided with a list of abbreviations to help you record your assignments quickly. The alphabetized list of abbreviations below is intended to help you save time when you are taking notes. You can also make up your own abbreviations. Space has been left for you to add to the list. Writing them down will help you remember them, and if you forget, you can always refer back to the list.

Note-Taking Abbreviations

abv	=	above	hsty	=	history	thru	=	through	2	=	to
aft	=	after	ht	=	height	tm	=	time	&	=	and
bf	=	before	inc	=	incomplete	t/o	=	through out	>	=	more than
bgn	=	begin	info	=	information	u	=	you	<	=	less than
blw	=	below	imp	=	important	un	=	unit	'	=	foot
cen	=	century	min	=	minute	v	=	very	"	=	inch
comp	=	complete	mny	=	many	w	=	with		=	
dur	=	during	mth	=	month	whn	=	when		=	
ex	=	example	n/t	=	next to	wht	=	what		=	
exer	=	exercise	nt	=	not	w/o	=	without		=	
fin	=	finish	ppl	=	people	wd	=	wide		=	
gd	=	good	prob	=	problem	wdth	=	width		=	
hr	=	hour	sec	=	section	yr	=	year		=	

Practicing Note-Taking

You are now going to use the information you highlighted or underlined in the first three paragraphs of the laser unit and put this information into standard note-taking form. Once you understand how to take notes, go back to the laser unit on page 93 and continue taking notes using the information you highlighted. As you can see on page 106, the key underlined information has been converted into standard notes. The first three underlined paragraphs are reproduced on the following page.

LASERS

Expanding the Frontiers of Science and Technology

Imagine a very narrow beam of light capable of drilling two hundred holes on a spot as tiny as the head of a pin and powerful enough to pierce a diamond, the hardest natural substance. This intense beam of light can be also be used to trigger a small nuclear reaction or to reach the moon more than 250,000 miles away.

In 1960, an American scientist named Theodore H. Maiman built a machine that could produce this intense light. He called his invention a laser. The word is an *acronym* whose letters stand for Light Amplification by Stimulated Emission of Radiation.

Types of Lasers

Today there are four main types of lasers: solid-state, semiconductor, gas-discharge, and dye lasers. These devices can range in size from as small as a grain of salt to as large as a football field.

Transforming Energy into Intense Light

Lasers typically have three main parts: an *energy source*, a substance called an *active medium* (also called a *resonator*), and a structure enclosing the active medium known as an *optical cavity*. The energy source typically supplies an electric current. The flash of energy is absorbed by the active medium. The atoms in the active medium--usually a gas or synthetic material--are excited, and the energy level increases. This energy is temporarily stored and then discharged in the form of light waves. Mirrors at the ends of the optical cavity reflect the light back into the active medium. More atoms are excited, and additional energy is produced. The light grows increasingly intense. The energy exits the laser as a narrow beam that may be visible, or invisible when the beam is comprised exclusively of radiation.

SAMPLE NOTES

Why are lasers expanding the frontiers of science and technology?

- Narrow beam light → drill 200 holes on spot tiny as pin head →pierce diamond, hardest nature substance → trigger small nuclear reaction → reach moon 250,000 miles away
- American scientist—Theodore H. Maiman - invented 1960
- Acronym: Light Amplification by Stimulated Emission Radiation

What are the types of lasers?

- size: grain salt → football field
- 4 types
- Gas-discharge
- Solid-state
- Semiconductor
- Dye

How do you transform energy into intense light?

- 3 main parts → energy source → active medium (resonator) → optical cavity enclosing active medium
- Energy source → electric current → energy absorbed by active medium (gas or synthetic material → atoms excited → energy level increases → energy temporarily stored → discharged as light waves → mirrors ends optical cavity reflect light back active medium → more atoms excited → additional energy produced → light grows increasingly intense
- Energy exits narrow beam → visible or invisible (radiation)

Copy these notes onto binder paper. Turn to the complete laser unit on page 93 and continue to take notes on your own using the information you've already highlighted. Remember to turn each subtitle into a question, indent, and copy only important information,

Mastery: More Practice Note-Taking

Use the **"Chewing-Up Information" Method** to take notes on the following history unit. Do Steps 1-3. Before you begin taking notes (Step 4), *look carefully at the sample Cleopatra notes on page 109*. ***Do not highlight or underline. Go directly to the note-taking step.***

After completing Steps 1 - 3, copy the sample notes on notebook paper. Then continue taking notes on the rest of the unit. Write neatly and indent. Your notes should look like the sample notes.

CLEOPATRA

One of the Most Fascinating Queens in History

More than two thousand years ago, an extraordinary young woman named Cleopatra ascended the throne in Egypt. Although portrayed in books and movies as being exceptionally beautiful, Cleopatra was actually quite plain. Her most striking qualities were her wit, charm, and intelligence. An historian of the period reported that Cleopatra could speak eight languages and described her as one of the most brilliant women of her time.

The Struggle for Power in Egypt

Cleopatra was the last in a dynasty (rulers of the same family) founded by a general named Ptolemy in 323 B.C. She became queen of Egypt in 51 B.C. when her father Ptolemy XII died. Only seventeen at the time, she was forced to share her power with her ten-year-old brother, Ptolemy XIII, who also became her husband. Such a marriage would be illegal today, but in Egyptian royal families during this era, marriage between a brother and sister was common.

The guardians of Ptolemy XIII wanted him to rule Egypt alone, and they plotted against Cleopatra. Successful in seizing power, they drove Cleopatra from the throne and forced her into exile.

In 48 B.C., a famous Roman general named Caesar invaded Egypt with his army and arrived in Alexandria, Egypt's capital. Caesar was pursuing a rival general named Pompey with whom he was struggling for power in Rome.

Realizing that Caesar could help her defeat Ptolemy and that he could help her regain the throne, Cleopatra decided to win Caesar's support. Because she was afraid he would not agree to see her, she supposedly hid herself in a carpet and had one of her servants carry the carpet to Caesar. Very impressed with Cleopatra's cleverness, Caesar agreed to help her. In 47 B.C., his army defeated Ptolemy's forces in battle. Ptolemy drowned while attempting to escape.

Caesar put Cleopatra back on the throne and fell in love with the young queen. In 46 B.C., Caesar invited Cleopatra to visit Rome. She accepted. Certain politicians in Rome feared that Caesar wanted to make himself king. To prevent this, they assassinated him in 44 B.C. on the steps of the Roman Senate.

Some historians believe that Cleopatra wanted to become Caesar's queen after he became king of the Roman Empire. She may have dreamed about joining the two kingdoms, but no one can be certain. If she did have a secret agenda, the plans disintegrated when Caesar was assassinated. Cleopatra realized that unless she returned to Egypt, she too might be killed.

Mark Antony

Mark Antony led an army against those responsible for the assassination of Caesar and defeated them. After the battle, three men shared power in Rome: Mark Antony, Lepidus, and Octavian, Caesar's nephew. These men became the rulers of the Roman Empire. Soon after Caesar's death, Mark Antony went to Asia Minor with his army.

Mark Antony had met Cleopatra during her stay in Rome. He wrote Cleopatra and asked her to visit him in Asia Minor. Wanting to rule Rome alone, he was hoping to obtain money from Cleopatra and to form an alliance against Caesar's nephew, Octavian.

Although she was unsure of his motives, the twenty-nine-year-old queen sailed from Alexandria to meet Mark Antony. Upon her arrival, she invited him to visit her aboard her magnificent royal barge. As Caesar had been before him, Mark Antony was captivated by Cleopatra's charm and wit. They fell in love. They were later married, and Cleopatra gave birth to twins, a boy and a girl.

The Civil War in Rome

While Mark Antony was in Asia Minor with Cleopatra, Octavian ruled Rome. Octavian believed that Mark Antony was the lovestruck victim of a wicked, greedy, and ambitious temptress and that he had had become her puppet. In 32 B.C., a civil war broke out for control of the Roman Empire. Octavian and Mark Antony were now bitter enemies.

Antony was an excellent general, but his army had been badly weakened during the conquest of Parthia. Historians have also suggested that Antony was spoiled by luxury and was no longer as talented as he had been during previous battles. In 31 B.C., the fleets of Mark Antony and Cleopatra were defeated when they were attacked off the coast of western Greece by Octavian's ships at the Battle of Actium.

The Return to Alexandria

Antony and Cleopatra fled with their remaining ships to Alexandria. Octavian pursued them and laid siege to the city. During this siege, thousands of Antony's soldiers deserted.

Cleopatra spread a false report that she had committed suicide. Antony learned of her supposed death. In despair, he attempted to kill himself by falling on his sword. Before he died, he found out that Cleopatra was actually still alive. He asked his followers to carry him to her. Barely alive, Antony begged Cleopatra to save herself. Soon after, he died in her arms.

When Cleopatra met with Octavian after Mark Antony's death, she tried to make peace with him, but she failed. Fearing Octavian would publicly humiliate and then murder her, she decided to commit suicide.

Cleopatra asked Octavian for permission to visit Mark Antony's tomb. In a basket of figs, she had hidden a small deadly snake called an asp. Taking the snake from the basket, she let it sink its fangs into her neck. When Octavian's soldiers returned, they found her dead by Antony's side. Cleopatra was thirty-nine years old.

The historian Plutarch reported that Octavian ordered a magnificent funeral for the two lovers. He also commanded that their bodies be placed side by side for people to see.

Many believe that Cleopatra failed because she was too ambitious. Certainly she captivated two of the greatest Romans of her era, Caesar and Mark Antony. She failed, however, to captivate another powerful Roman, and this man destroyed her. His name was Octavian.

SAMPLE NOTES

Why was Cleopatra one of the most remarkable queens in history?

Why was there a struggle for power in Egypt?

- Cleopatra ruled Egypt → more than 2,000 yrs. ago
- Not beautiful → witty, charming, intelligent
- Last of dynasty founded by Ptolemy
- Queen at 17 in 51 B.C. → had to share power *w* younger brother Ptolemy XIII → married
- P's guardians plotted against Cleo → took away power & forced her exile
- Roman general Caesar came to Egypt army in 48 B.C.
- C. agreed to help Cleo → his army defeated P → P drowned → Cleo queen in 47 B.C.
- Fell in love → invited Cleo to Rome in 46 B.C.

- Politicians in Rome feared C wanted to become king → assassinated him
- Cleo returned Egypt

Who was Mark Antony?

- Friend Caesar
- Led army against C's killers

After you have copied the sample notes, continue taking notes on your own. Remember to write neatly. If you use abbreviations, make sure you understand them! Leave out information you do not think is important. For example, the information about the carpet may be interesting, but most teachers would probably not ask you about it on a test. There is too much other information in the unit that they would most likely consider more important.

When you have completed taking notes, compare your notes with the completed model notes. If you have left information out, add it to your notes.

COMPLETED MODEL NOTES

Why was Cleopatra one of the most remarkable queens in history?

Why was there a struggle for power in Egypt?

- Cleopatra ruled Egypt → 2,000 yrs. ago
- Not beautiful → witty, charming, bright
- Last of dynasty founded by Ptolemy
- Queen at 17 in 51 B.C. → had to share power *w* younger brother Ptolemy XIII → married
- P's guardians plotted against Cleo→ took away power & forced her exile
- Roman General Caesar came to Egypt army in 48 B.C. → pursuing rival general Pompey
- C. agreed to help Cleo → his army defeated P → P drowned → Cleo queen in 47 B.C.
- Fell in love → invited Cleo to Rome in 46 B.C.
- Politicians Rome feared C. wanted to become king → assassinated him
- Cleo returned Egypt

Who was Mark Antony?

- Friend Caesar
- Led army against C's killers
- Ruled Roman Empire with Lepidus and Octavian
- M.A. went to Asia Minor w army

- Met Cleo. → form alliance against Octavian
- Fell in love →married → had twins

Why was there a civil war in Rome?

- Octavian ruled Rome while M.A. away
- Octvn. tried to seize power
- Civil war to control empire → M.A. & Octvn. became enemies
- Octvn. defeated M.A. & Cleo's fleets--Battle of Actium 31 B.C.

Why did they return to Alexandria?

- Cleo and M.A. fled defeat
- Octavian laid siege to city
- Thousands of M.A.'s soldiers deserted
- M.A. heard Cleo had committed suicide → not true
- M.A. fell on sword → badly wounded
- M.A. died in Cleo's arms
- Cleo afraid public humiliation and murder by Octvn
- Cleo asked Octvn. to visit M.A.'s tomb
- Committed suicide using asp
- Octvn. ordered magnificent funeral

Answering Essay Questions

It's now time to do the last two steps of the **"Chewing-Up Information" Method.**

STEP 5: Answer the *subtitle* questions. Write each question on a piece of paper. Skip a space and begin writing your answer. Write powerful complete sentences that summarize the information. Remember to put the subtitle question at the top of the paper. You may use your notes to answer the subtitle questions.

You want to begin each short essay with a *strong topic sentence.* A sample topic sentence is found below. You may use this sample when you answer the first subtitle question, or you can make up your own.

Sample Topic Sentence

Cleopatra became queen of Egypt when she was 17, but she was forced to share power with her younger brother, Ptolemy XIII.

When you have written your essay and have included all the information that is important, you will then need to write a strong concluding sentence. This sentence should tie the information together and summarize the information you have written in the essay. You may use the sample concluding sentence below or write your own.

Sample Concluding Sentence

After Caesar was killed, Cleopatra feared that she, too, might be assassinated, and she decided to return to Egypt.

Answering Subtitle Questions

Why was there a struggle for power in Egypt?

____

____

____

____

____

____

____

Who was Mark Antony?

______

______

______

______

______

______

Why was there a civil war in Rome?

______

______

______

______

______

______

Why did Cleopatra and Mark Antony return to Alexandria?

______

______

______

______

______

Answering the Title Question

STEP 6: Answer the title question: ***"Why was Cleopatra one of the most fascinating queens in history?"***

You want your essay to demonstrate clearly that you understand the content and recall the important information. For this exercise, you may use your notes to answer the title question, or you may choose to answer the question without using your notes. If this question were actually asked on a test, the teacher would probably not allow you to use notes. You would have to include as much as you could remember from having taken notes and from having studied the material.

When teachers grade an essay, they base their evaluation on content, organization, and writing skills. Before beginning to answer a test essay question, it is a good idea to jot down quickly in outline form the key points you want to make. You can do this in pencil and then erase it before handing in the test, or you can use a separate piece of paper. Your outline should be *very* brief, and should take no more than a minute or two to do. Because it is very small, this type of outline is called a "thumb-nail" outline. A sample thumb-nail outline is found below.

Question: Why was there a struggle for power in Egypt?

Sample Thumb-Nail Outline:

Queen at 17 – 51 B.C.

Forced share power with P

Married P

P's guardian wanted him have power

Cleo forced exile

C. helped Cleo → defeated P → P drowned

Cleo. → ascended throne

When you take an essay test and write an important essay, your thumb-nail outline will remind you to include the important information. It will also help you organize your thoughts. Teachers like clear, well-organized essays, and they give students who write them good grades!

Now it's time to answer the title question. Write your essay on a separate piece of paper. Because you should include *all* the key information, this essay will be longer than the subtitle essays. For practice, write the essay *without looking at your notes*. Since you will have more time on a test to answer a main-idea question, you will have time to do a quick thumb-nail outline. Include all the facts you think your teacher would consider important. Organize the information so that it makes sense and "flows." Your goal is to impress your teacher with how much you know about Cleopatra. Remember: begin with a strong topic sentence. A sample is found on the next page.

Sample Topic Sentence for Title Question Essay

Over two thousand years ago, a remarkable 17-year-old woman became queen of Egypt

When you finish your essay, you will want to tie everything together with a strong concluding statement. Once you complete the essay, compare it and the others you wrote with the models below. Your essays do not have to be the same. They will be written in your own words, and they may actually be better than the models! It's very important that your essays contain the important information and that you start each with a powerful topic sentence and end with a powerful concluding sentence. You will also need to proofread your essays carefully so that you find spelling and grammatical mistakes. After reading the model essays, you may want to make changes or additions in your own essays. If you want to write effectively, you must continually work at improving your skills. Good writing requires practice, effort, and many revisions!

Model Essays

Subtitle Questions:

Why was there a struggle for power in Egypt?

Cleopatra became queen of Egypt when she was 17, but she was forced to share power with her brother, Ptolemy. Her brother's guardians plotted against her and forced her into exile. The Roman general Caesar was pursuing a rival general named Pompey. He came to Egypt with an army, and he agreed to help Cleopatra. His forces defeated Ptolemy's forces, and Cleopatra assumed the throne

Who was Mark Antony?

Caesar was assassinated in Rome. His friend Mark Antony led an army against the killers. After defeating them, Mark Antony, Octavian, and Lepidus ruled the Roman Empire. Later Mark Antony went to Asia Minor with an army, and he and Cleopatra formed an alliance against Octavian. They also fell in love.

Why was there a civil war in Rome?

Octavian, who was the ruler in Rome while Mark Antony was in Egypt, tried to seize power. Octavian was convinced that Mark Antony was being controlled by Cleopatra. He and Mark Antony became enemies. Mark Antony's army had become weak, and Octavian's fleet defeated Cleopatra and Mark Antony at the Battle of Actium in 31 B.C.

Why did they return to Alexandria?

After their defeat by Octavian's fleet, Mark Antony and Cleopatra fled back to Alexandria. Octavian's forces laid siege, and many of Antony's soldiers deserted. Mark Antony heard an untrue report that Cleopatra had died. He tried to kill himself. When he learned that she was alive, he had his men take him to her. He died in her arms, and she committed suicide.

Title Question: **Why Was Cleopatra One of the Most Fascinating Queens in History?**

Cleopatra was a very smart woman. She wanted to rule Egypt and was able to win over powerful people who could help her achieve her goal. First she persuaded Caesar to help her defeat her brother, Ptolemy XIII. Later, she persuaded Mark Antony to join forces with her. Together they tried to defeat Mark Antony's enemies in Rome. Their plan failed, and they were defeated. Despite this failure, Cleopatra must still be considered a remarkable queen. She was willing to reach for her goals, and she almost succeeded.

Distinguishing Main Ideas from Details

After you have completed taking notes and have answered the subtitle and main-idea questions, review your notes at least one time before taking a test. A good review technique is to read through your notes and to use highlight pens to indicate which information is a main idea and which information is a detail. For example, "had to share power with younger brother" is a main idea. It is a main idea because much of what happened to Cleopatra was the result of the power struggle with Ptolemy's guardians. Examples of details include "ruled over 2,000 years ago," "Queen at 17," and Battle Actium in 31 B.C.

Make sure that you have two highlight pens in different colors. Use one color for details and one for main ideas. If you do not have highlighters, use a pencil to underline details and a pen to underline main ideas. Review your notes and highlight or underline the main ideas and details.

As an added review, you should write each main idea on one side of an index card and the relevant details about the main idea on the other side of the index card. When you study, look at each main idea and then see how many details you can remember. By simply flipping over the card, you can check to make sure you have recalled the key details. This procedure will take extra time, but if it helps you get a good grade, the extra work will be worth it.

Side 1 of Sample Index Card: Main Idea

Cleopatra Involved in Power Struggle with Younger Brother Ptolemy XIII

Side 2 of Sample Index Card: Relevant Details

Cleopatra last in dynasty
Ruled more than 2000 years ago
Forced to share power with Ptolemy XIII
At 17, became Queen in 51 B.C.
In 48 B.C., Roman general Caesar helped Cleo. regain throne

Remembering the "Chewing-Up Information" Method

You might find it easier to remember the seven steps of the "Chewing-Up Information" Method by memorizing the first letter of each step. To help you remember the steps, just recall a person's name: **MISS RC NAR.**

MI Main-Idea Question
S Subtitle Questions
S Speed-Read
RC Read Carefully
N Notes
A Answer Subtitle and Main-Idea Questions
R Review

What I Have Learned about the "Chewing-Up Information" Method

	True	False
I should turn the title into question before reading the material.	____	_____
I should turn each subtitle into a question before reading the material.	____	_____
I should try to answer the title question before reading the material.	____	_____
I should try to answer the subtitle questions before taking notes.	____	_____
I should speed-read the material after posing main-idea question.	____	_____
I should read every word very carefully when I speed-read.	____	_____
After speed-reading, I should read the material again more carefully.	____	_____
I should write down key information in note form as I read carefully.	____	_____
I should include words such as "the," "a," and "of" in my notes.	____	_____
I should use abbreviations whenever possible.	____	_____
I should highlight or underline in my textbooks.	____	_____
It is not all that important that I be able to recall my abbreviations.	____	_____
Notes taken from textbooks should be written in paragraph form.	____	_____
It is smart to review notes carefully and indicate main ideas and details.	____	_____
It is smart to write each main idea on one side of an index card and the details on the other side.	____	_____
It is smart to use the index cards to review before a test.	____	_____

What I Have Learned about Answering Essay Questions

	True	False
The last step is to write an essay that answers the title question.	____	_____
Before writing a test essay, I should make a quick thumb-nail outline, to organize the information and make certain that I include the key points.	____	_____
I should always write a strong topic sentence.	____	_____
The concluding sentence is not as important as the topic sentence.	____	_____

Unit 9

Studying for Tests

Developing a Test-Preparation Strategy

On Monday Kelly's history teacher announced that there would be a unit test on Friday. He said that the test would take the entire period and would consist of twenty multiple-choice questions, twenty true/false questions, twenty short-answer questions, and one essay.

Kelly carefully noted the information on the assignment sheet that she kept in the front of her binder. Despite having already read the material and having taken notes in class, she still felt apprehensive. Tests always made her anxious. Since elementary school, she feared that she would not know the answers because she had studied the wrong material or that she wouldn't be able to remember what she had learned.

Kelly realized that her test anxiety was probably linked to the learning difficulties that had made her life miserable in elementary school. But she was now a good reader. She was no longer in the resource program, and she was doing well in her classes. In fact, she had a 3.2 grade-point-average, and this made her very proud. Test anxiety, however, was still a problem. Fortunately, her fear usually melted away once the test was finally handed to her, and she could concentrate on answering the questions.

In preparing for the test, Kelly speed-read the unit, and she then carefully re-read the material. She spent an additional two hours mind-mapping and taking notes. Because getting a good grade was very important to her, she didn't mind making the extra effort. She targeted getting at least a B+ on the test, but she was really hoping for an A-. This would mover her close to achieving her goals: graduating from high school with a 3.4 GPA; attending the state university, and earning a degree in special education so that she could help kids who are struggling in school.

It was time for Kelly to put her final test-preparation strategy into action. On Monday night, she reviewed her notes and answered the subtitle questions and main-idea title question. She made sure that her essays were well-organized. She began each essay with a strong topic sentence and ended each with a strong concluding sentence. Kelly had budgeted an hour of study time to do this, and she had kept to her schedule.

On Tuesday night, Kelly reviewed her notes again. She used colored highlight pens and marked the main ideas in blue and the details in yellow. She then wrote each main idea on one side of a large index card, and she wrote the relevant details on the other side. She had budgeted an hour of study time, but she only needed 50 minutes to complete this stage of her study plan.

On Wednesday evening, Kelly used the memory technique her teacher had shown the class to help her memorize the important facts, names, and dates she had written on the back of each of the index cards. This required 45 minutes. She had budgeted an hour, so she had fifteen extra minutes to spend on writing her book report.

On Thursday evening, Kelly made up a practice test that consisted of multiple-choice, short-answer, and true/false test questions. She made sure that she could answer all of the questions. Then she called Stephanie, and she and her friend spent forty minutes asking each other questions about the unit. These final test preparation steps required an hour and forty-five minutes. This was thirty minutes more than she had budgeted, but she didn't mind. When they had finished asking each other questions, Kelly still felt anxious about the test, but she also felt confident. She had done everything she could do to prepare. She was ready!

Learning How to Study Effectively for a Test

Your final preparation before a test is critically important! These steps can make the difference between getting a good grade and getting a poor grade.

Let's review the studying techniques you have already learned. You now know how to:

1. **Record assignments accurately**
2. **Create a quiet and non-distracting study environment**
3. **Calculate and budget adequate study time**
4. **Speed-read**

5. **Mind-map**
6. **Ask title and subtitle questions**
7. **Take notes**
8. **Answer title and subtitle questions**
9. **Study your notes**
10. **Write each main idea on one side of an index card and details on the other**

There are *three additional important steps* you can take:

11. **Carefully consider what your teacher is likely to regard as important and spend extra time reviewing this information**
12. **Make up and answer practice test questions**
13. **Do a final test review with a friend and ask each other questions**

Teachers have different preferences for what they want their students to learn. Those who want you to learn facts might ask the following types of detail questions on a test:

- *When did Cleopatra become queen of Egypt?*
- *When did Caesar invade Egypt?*
- *Who ruled Rome while Marc Antony was in Egypt?*
- *When was the Battle of Actium?*

Other teachers want you to understand and remember the main ideas. On an essay test, they might ask: *"Why is Cleopatra considered one of the most remarkable women is history?"*

If your teacher asks a great many detail questions on tests, it would be smart to make up a list of important details when you study. As you have already highlighted details in your notes with different colors, you could easily make up the list and write the details on index cards. You could then focus on memorizing these facts. You could review the index cards whenever you have a free moment—on the school bus, during lunch, or in study hall. This would, of course, require extra time, but it would certainly improve your chances of getting a better grade on a detail-oriented test.

Once you identify the important facts in your notes, you have to figure out a method for remembering these facts. Unless you have a great memory, reading over the list a few times is not enough. To memorize information easily, you'll need to learn powerful memory techniques. These techniques are taught later in this unit.

A Final Test-Preparation Template

A template is a guide or an overlay that you place over something to make sure the measurements are accurate. A powerful test-preparation template can be added to your arsenal of study skills. It's simple and easy to remember, and if you use it, you should be able to improve your performance on tests.

There are four steps in the template. You can remember the steps by using the acronym **ICRA.** This acronym is formed from the first letter of each of the four steps:

Identify, Comprehend, Remember, and Anticipate.

Let's take a look at the template.

Identify: You should identify the information that you think is important, as well as the information that you believe your teacher would consider important. Teachers usually give hints about what they want you to learn. They may give out a study guide, or they may indicate that something is important during a class discussion or when they are lecturing in class. *(You are also identifying what you believe is important when you take notes, highlight details and main ideas, and ask yourself test review questions.)*

Comprehend: To do well on tests, you must *understand* what you're studying. Memorizing information is always easier when you understand the content. *(You do this step when you mind-map and use the "Chewing-Up Information" Method.)*

Remember: Once you identify and understand the important information, you must use effective memory techniques to recall the information. *(These techniques are taught later in this unit.)*

Anticipate: By thinking like a teacher when you study and by figuring out the questions your teacher is likely to ask on a test, you have an advantage over students who don't anticipate likely questions when they study.

You've already learned how to ***identify*** and ***understand*** important information. In the following sections of this unit, you are going to learn how to memorize the information (the **R**emember step) and how to make up tests (the **A**nticipate step).

For this activity you are going to do the steps out of order, and you are going to start with the making-up-tests step. The Cleopatra unit is reprinted below, and you will use it to make up different types of practice test questions.

CLEOPATRA

One of the Most Fascinating Queens in History

More than two thousand years ago, an extraordinary young woman named Cleopatra ascended the throne in Egypt. Although portrayed in books and movies as being exceptionally beautiful, Cleopatra was actually quite plain. Her most striking qualities were her wit, charm, and intelligence. An historian of the period reported that Cleopatra could speak eight languages and described her as one of the most brilliant women of her time.

The Struggle for Power in Egypt

Cleopatra was the last in a dynasty (rulers of the same family) founded by a general named Ptolemy in 323 B.C. She became queen of Egypt in 51 B.C. when her father Ptolemy XII died. Only seventeen at the time, she was forced to share her power with her ten-year-old brother, Ptolemy XIII, who also became her husband. Such a marriage would be illegal today, but in Egyptian royal families during this era, marriage between a brother and sister was common.

The guardians of Ptolemy XIII wanted him to rule Egypt alone, and they plotted against Cleopatra. Successful in seizing power, they drove Cleopatra from the throne and forced her into exile.

In 48 B.C., a famous Roman general named Caesar invaded Egypt with his army and arrived in Alexandria, Egypt's capital. Caesar was pursuing a rival general named Pompey with whom he was struggling for power in Rome.

Realizing that Caesar could help her defeat Ptolemy and that he could help her regain the throne, Cleopatra decided to win Caesar's support. Because she was afraid he would not agree to see her, she supposedly hid herself in a carpet and had one of her servants carry the carpet to

Caesar. Very impressed with Cleopatra's cleverness, Caesar agreed to help her. In 47 B.C., his army defeated Ptolemy's forces in battle. Ptolemy drowned while attempting to escape.

Caesar put Cleopatra back on the throne and fell in love with the young queen. In 46 B.C., Caesar invited Cleopatra to visit Rome. She accepted. Certain politicians in Rome feared that Caesar wanted to make himself king. To prevent this, they assassinated him in 44 B.C. on the steps of the Roman senate.

Some historians believe that Cleopatra wanted to become Caesar's queen after he became king of the Roman Empire. She may have dreamed about joining the two kingdoms, but no one can be certain. If she did have a secret agenda, the plans disintegrated when Caesar was assassinated. Cleopatra realized that unless she returned to Egypt, she too might be killed.

Mark Antony

Mark Antony led an army against those responsible for the assassination of Caesar and defeated them. After the battle, three men shared power in Rome: Mark Antony, Lepidus, and Octavian, Caesar's nephew. These men became the rulers of the Roman Empire. Soon after Caesar's death, Mark Antony went to Asia Minor with his army.

Mark Antony had met Cleopatra during her stay in Rome. He wrote Cleopatra and asked her to visit him in Asia Minor. Wanting to rule Rome alone, he was hoping to obtain money from Cleopatra and to form an alliance against Caesar's nephew, Octavian.

Although she was unsure of his motives, the twenty-nine-year-old queen sailed from Alexandria to meet Mark Antony. Upon her arrival, she invited him to visit her aboard her magnificent royal barge. As Caesar had been before him, Mark Antony was captivated by Cleopatra's charm and wit. They fell in love. They were later married, and Cleopatra gave birth to twins, a boy and a girl.

The Civil War in Rome

While Mark Antony was in Asia Minor with Cleopatra, Octavian ruled Rome. Octavian believed that Mark Antony was the lovestruck victim of a wicked, greedy, and ambitious temptress and that he had become her puppet. In 32 B.C., a civil war broke out for control of the Roman Empire. Octavian and Mark Antony were now bitter enemies.

Antony was an excellent general, but his army had been badly weakened during the conquest of Parthia. Historians have also suggested that Antony was spoiled by luxury and was no longer as talented as he had been during previous battles. In 31 B.C., the fleets of Mark Antony and Cleopatra were defeated when they were attacked off the coast of western Greece by Octavian's ships at the Battle of Actium.

The Return to Alexandria

Antony and Cleopatra fled with their remaining ships to Alexandria. Octavian pursued them and laid siege to the city. During this siege, thousands of Antony's soldiers deserted.

Cleopatra spread a false report that she had committed suicide. Antony learned of her supposed death. In despair, he attempted to kill himself by falling on his sword. Before he died, he found out that Cleopatra was actually still alive. He asked his followers to carry him to her. Barely alive, Antony begged Cleopatra to save herself. Soon after, he died in her arms.

When Cleopatra met with Octavian after Mark Antony's death, she tried to make peace with him, but she failed. Fearing Octavian would publicly humiliate and then murder her, she decided to commit suicide.

Cleopatra asked Octavian for permission to visit Mark Antony's tomb. In a basket of figs, she had hidden a small deadly snake called an asp. Taking the snake from the basket, she let it sink its fangs into her neck. When Octavian's soldiers returned, they found her dead by Antony's side. Cleopatra was thirty-nine years old.

The historian Plutarch reported that Octavian ordered a magnificent funeral for the two lovers. He also commanded that their bodies be placed side by side for people to see.

Many believe that Cleopatra's failed because she was too ambitious. Certainly she captivated two of the greatest Romans of her era, Caesar and Mark Antony. She failed, however, to captivate another powerful Roman, and this man destroyed her. His name was Octavian.

Making Up and Answering Short-Answer Questions

Now use the details from the unit to make up fifteen short-answer questions. For example:

When did Cleopatra become queen of Egypt?

When did Caesar invade Egypt?

Short-Answer/Detail Questions

1. ____________________
2. ____________________
3. ____________________
4. ____________________
5. ____________________
6. ____________________
7. ____________________
8. ____________________
9. ____________________
10. ____________________
11. ____________________
12. ____________________
13. ____________________
14. ____________________
15. ____________________

Now answer your own questions!

Answers

1. ____________________
____
2. ____________________
____
3. ____________________
____
4. ____________________
____
5. ____________________
____
6. ____________________
____

7. ____

____

8. ____

____

9. ____

____

10. ____

____

11. ____

____

12. ____

____

13. ____

____

14. ____

____

15. ____

____

Making Up and Answering True/False Questions

Teachers who want you to know facts and information often ask true/false questions on tests. Make up 15 true/false questions from the Cleopatra unit. If you want, you can change the short-answer questions you made so that they are now true/false questions. For example:

Mark Antony invaded Egypt with his army in 48 BC. True False

True/False Questions

1. ____

True False

2. ____

True False

3. ____

True False

4. ____

True False

5. ____

True False

6. ____

True False

7. ____

True False

8. ____

True False

9. ____

True False

10. ____

True False

11. ____

True False

12. ____

True False

13. ____

True False

14. ____

True False

15. ____

True False

Now answer your own questions!

Making Up and Answering Multiple-Choice Questions

Make up 10 multiple-choice questions from the Cleopatra unit. For example:

Cleopatra ruled Egypt:

a. 4000 years ago **c. 3000 years ago**

b. in the 1st century **d. 2000 years ago**

Multiple-Choice Questions

1. ______________________________:
    a. ______________________
    b. ______________________
    c. ______________________
    d. ______________________
2. ______________________________:
    a. ______________________
    b. ______________________
    c. ______________________
    d. ______________________
3. ______________________________:
    a. ______________________
    b. ______________________
    c. ______________________
    d. ______________________
4. ______________________________:
    a. ______________________
    b. ______________________
    c. ______________________
    d. ______________________
5. ______________________________:
    a. ______________________
    b. ______________________
    c. ______________________
    d. ______________________
6. ______________________________:
    a. ______________________
    b. ______________________
    c. ______________________
    d. ______________________

7. ____:

   a. ____

   b. ____

   c. ____

   d. ____

8. ____:

   a. ____

   b. ____

   c. ____

   d. ____

9. ____:

   a. ____

   b. ____

   c. ____

   d. ____

10. ____:

   a. ____

   b. ____

   c. ____

   d. ____

Now go back and answer your own questions!

Working Back from Multiple-Choice Answers

Good students often use a trick when they take a multiple-choice test. If they aren't sure what the correct answer is, they will look at each of the possible answers and try to rule out those that are obviously wrong and those that are probably wrong. This might eliminate two or more of the choices. They may be left with only one answer, and they will circle it. It's also possible that they may be left with two answers that could be correct. If they have to guess, they have at least increased the odds of selecting the correct answer because they have eliminated two choices. Let's look at how this method works.

To escape Octavian, Mark Antony and Cleopatra sailed with their remaining ships to:

a. Rome **c. Alexandria**

b. Cairo **d. Paris**

Let's examine the four choices. Paris is a city in France, and nothing in the unit referred to France. So this answer could be eliminated. Rome also doesn't makes sense. If Cleopatra and Mark Antony were trying to escape Octavian, they certainly wouldn't go to Rome which was the capital of the country they were fighting. So Rome can be eliminated. This leaves only two choices: Cairo and Alexandria. You may realize that Cairo was not mentioned in the unit. You may also recall that Alexandria was mentioned. If you do not remember this, you may have to guess and choose either answer b or c. If you do have to guess, you have increased the chances of getting the correct answer from one out of four to one out of two possibilities.

This method of ruling out the wrong answers to help you find the right answer can be very valuable when you aren't certain of the correct answer. Try the method the next time you take a multiple-choice test.

Jolting Your Memory

Have you ever thought about how many things you are expected to memorize? Let's look at some examples:

- Your home telephone number
- Your address
- Your locker number
- Your parents' work telephone numbers
- The combination to your bike lock
- The Pledge of Allegiance
- The multiplication tables
- The name of the first President of the United States
- The three branches of government
- The spelling of the word "receive"

You may not even realize that you are continually memorizing information in school. You have read about George Washington so many times that you know he was the first President of the United States without thinking about it.

Sometimes you have to make an effort to memorize information. The multiplication tables are a perfect example. When you were in third grade, you had to practice and recite the tables over and over until you learned them. You had to memorize that 7 x 8 = 56. If you did not memorize your multiplication tables, you could not do short- and long-division problems. You would not be able to divide 7 into 56 and know that the correct answer is 8.

There are different ways to help you memorize information. Some of the most common methods include:

- **Writing information over and over until you memorize it**
- **Reciting information aloud over and over many times until you memorize it**
- **Re-reading material until you memorize it**
- **Making a picture or word association to help you memorize the information**

You've probably already used the first three methods for remembering information. Let's take a look at the last technique, **making an association.** This method may be of great help when you have to memorize spelling words, multiplication tables, or facts in a textbook or in your notes. In the section below, you will learn how to use this tool.

Making Powerful Associations

Look at the following definitions and sample sentences:

attain to achieve

His next goal was to ***attain*** *a college degree so that he could go to law school and become an attorney.*

peruse: to examine

She loved to ***peruse*** *the new books at her favorite bookstore.*

porous: having many holes

A sponge can hold a great deal of water because it is very ***porous.***

reign: the rule of a king or queen

During the King Edward's ***reign****, there was much suffering.*

expedition: a trip of exploration

Because they loved travel and adventure, they decided to take an ***expedition*** *to Africa and film wild animals.*

A good way to remember these words is to make an association (or connection) and then to "see" the word, the definition, and the association in your mind. This linking of a word and its definition is called the **Association/Visualization Technique**. Let's practice the technique.

Association/Visualization Technique

Step 1: Write the word and the definition to each word on a file card or on a piece of paper. Put only one word and its definition on each card. To help you form a visual picture, experiment writing the word in one color and the definition in a different color felt pen or pencil. You can also write the letters in each word in several different colors. Use as many colors as you like. You may decide to use one color for the word and another color for all definitions. Select the color combination that you like best.

Step 2: After writing down the word and the definition, tape or tack the card slightly above eye level slightly to either the right or the left. Keep looking at the word and its definition until you can actually "see" in your mind the word and its definition. Close your eyes and actually visualize the letters of the word and the definition in color on the *insides of your eyelids*. If you can't remember the definition, open your eyes and study the card again. When you're ready, try to see the word and definition again in your mind. This technique will help you imprint the information on your brain.

Step 3: Once you can see the definition in your mind, try to create a mental picture that uses the word and the image. For example, visualize a young adult being given a diploma at a graduation ceremony. In your mind, see this person showing her diploma to her parents and being proud that she has **attained** her goal. Or visualize a person in a bookstore happily **perusing** the newly released books that have been placed on a table at the entrance to the bookstore. Choose a powerful image to help you "take a picture" of the scene and remember the meaning of the word.

Step 4: Once you can see the word, the definition, and the visual image that uses the word and helps you remember the definition, write the word and the definition on a piece of lined paper without looking at the card. Then write the sentence that uses the word. Say the sentence aloud as you write it. Follow the same procedure with the next word and definition.

Taping or tacking the index card slightly above your head can be very effective in helping you use the visualization technique properly. You can recall visual information better when your eyes look up slightly. In this way your eyes are functioning like the lens of a camera and your brain is functioning like a role of film. The procedure helps you imprint the picture in your mind. Experiment with taping the card slightly to the left or the right of your nose **above eye level**. See whether the card "feels" better to the right or the left of your eyes.

This information-linking visualization method is effective with anything you have to memorize. This includes definitions, spelling words, formulas, dates, and number facts. Always choose a color you like. When studying vocabulary or spelling words, make up a sentence and an image you can easily visualize. (For example: A sweating athlete in a gym working <u>**strenuously**</u> as he lifts weights above his head.) The more vivid (realistic with many details), the more effective the mental image will be in helping you remember the information.

Now try another experiment. Use the **Association/Visualization** technique with the following spelling words. After you have used the method and feel you have learned the words, test yourself to see if you have remembered how to spell them.

correction	**porridge**	**masquerade**	**invisible**
misspell	**granddad**	**teammate**	**allegiance**
imprecise	**antique**	**lieutenant**	**sergeant**

Although you cannot make the same type of visual associations with math facts, you can still use the visualizing method. You can close your eyes and see 5 X 5 = 25 in your mind in color. Let's try one more experiment. Use the technique to help you remember the following difficult multiplication facts.

11 x 11 = 121	**12 x 12 = 144**	**13 x 13 = 169**	**14 x 14 = 196**	**15 x 15 = 225**
16 x 16 = 256	**17 x 17 = 309**	**18 x 18 = 324**	**19 x 19 = 361**	**20 x 20 = 400**

Now try the method with these chemical symbols.

H_2O	=	**water**
CO	=	**carbon monoxide (produced by a car engine)**
CO_2	=	**carbon dioxide (produced by lungs when we breathe)**
Na	=	**sodium**
Fe	=	**iron**
Pb	=	**lead**
H_2SO_4	=	**sulfuric acid**
HCl	=	**nitric acid**

Making Up Tests

You may think that making up a good test is an easy job for your teachers. Actually, it can be very difficult. Producing a fair history or science exam requires time and thought on the teacher's part. Let's look at what issues the teacher must consider.

1. **What is the important information in this unit?**
2. **What do I want my students to understand and remember?**
3. **How can I find out if my students have understood and retained the important information?**
4. **How can I ask challenging and fair questions that measure my students' knowledge and skills?**

If you can train yourself to *think like your teacher* when you study, you can increase the likelihood that you will anticipate what the teacher is likely to ask on a test. This gives you an advantage over kids who don't know how to identify the information that their teacher probably considers important.

If you think about it, you actually know a great deal about your teacher. You have spent lots of time together in the classroom. From hints in class and from past tests, you could probably guess what the teacher is going to ask on a test covering the Laser or Cleopatra unit.

There is one more powerful studying "trick" you can use to prepare for tests. This trick is very simple: **Make Up Your Own Test!** This should be the final step after you've completed your studying. On pages 126-130, you made up short-answer, true/false, and multiple-choice questions about the Cleopatra unit. To make up these questions, you had to go through each paragraph of the unit carefully. You may have also used your notes and your mind-map. Go back to the question you made up on pages 126-130. Think about the type of questions your teacher typically asks and select the test questions that you think *your* teacher would probably ask. On a separate piece of paper make a practice test of twenty-five different questions. For example:

Sample Practice Test Questions

1. When did Cleopatra live? ____________________
2. List three of Cleopatra's most remarkable qualities.

   ____

   ____

   ____
3. Cleopatra became queen at 14. **True** **False**
4. The name of Cleopatra's brother was: ____________________
5. Caesar helped Cleopatra's brother defeat Cleopatra's forces. **True** **False**
6. Marc Antony plotted against Caesar and had him assassinated on the steps of the Roman senate. **True** **False**
7. Caesar decided to help Cleopatra because:

   a. He wanted to become king of Egypt

   b. He was impressed with her.

   c. Ptolemy was plotting against him.

You can use these sample test questions as a model for making up your own test questions, but try not to use the exact same questions. You can, however, use some or all of the short-answer, multiple-choice, and true/false questions you made-up on pages 126-130. As you create the test, try to imagine what information your teacher would probably want you to know.

The Value of Thinking Like a Teacher

Teachers must go through the same process you just went through when making up a test. If you get in the habit of thinking like your teacher and you make up practice tests, your test performance should improve.

When you take a test, you may discover questions that you did not anticipate. Try to figure out why the teacher considered this particular information important. The next time you study, make adjustments and "fine-tune" your test preparation "radar."

Students who think about what they are studying and about what they need to learn are rarely surprised when they take a test. Usually they know in advance many of the questions that their teacher will ask.

Being Relaxed When You Take Tests

Some students do an excellent job of studying, but panic when they take tests. Because of their fear and anxiety, their grades do not reflect how much they have learned and how much time they spent preparing.

Taking a test can cause stress and anxiety for anyone, and it can be especially stressful if you really want to do well but have doubts about your skills or ability. You may have had difficulty taking tests in the past, and you may be convinced you cannot do well on them. As you wait for the teacher to hand out the test, your fear intensifies. Then you look at the test, and your brain "shuts down." You see questions you should be able to answer, but you think that the questions cover material you haven't studied. The questions may be slightly different from what you expected, and you are thrown into a panic and forget much of what you know.

In an extreme case, becoming stressed and going into a panic before taking a test can cause you to fail the test. In a less extreme case, you may get a C- instead of the B or B+ you deserve. If you prepared properly for the test, this would be unfair. All of your hard work could be undermined, and you would not be able to demonstrate what your really know.

There are four practical steps that can reduce your fear and stress before taking a test.

Test-Relaxation Techniques

- Close your eyes and *slowly* take several deep breaths while waiting for the test to be handed out. (Do not take more than 2 or 3 breaths as this may cause you to become dizzy.)
- Keep your eyes closed and form a picture in your mind of you looking at the questions, knowing the answers, taking the test, doing well, and feeling proud and confident.
- Silently recite and repeat positive statements about doing well while you are studying and when you are waiting for the test to be handed out.
- With your eyes closed, feel your body relax and feel the fear and stress flowing out of you.

Make it a habit to go through these steps when you take tests. As you begin to do better on tests as a result of your new study skills, your stress and fear should decrease.

Test-Preparation Checklist

As you begin to study for a test, use the following checklist. It will help you decide if you are preparing properly. If you do everything on this checklist, you can feel confident that you are well-prepared. You are thinking smart, and you have turbo-charged your studying. The methods you have learned require additional time at first, but the payoffs—good grades, pride, self-confidence—will make the extra time and effort worthwhile.

Each time you use the study power methods, your studying will become easier and more productive. Learning to study is like learning to ice skate. The more time you spend skating, the better your skills will become. With practice, desire, and effort, you will become a *"pro"* at preparing for tests.

Test-Preparation Checklist

	Yes	No
I accurately recorded information about the test on my assignment sheet.	___	___
I have allowed enough time to prepare for the test.	___	___
I made up a study schedule.	___	___
I kept to my study schedule.	___	___
I have studied in a quiet environment.	___	___
Before reading the material, I developed questions from the title and from each subtitle.	___	___
I have speed-read (skimmed) the material at least once.	___	___
I have mind-mapped and/or taken notes.	___	___
I have answered the subtitle and main-idea questions.	___	___
I have identified the main ideas and details in my notes.	___	___
I have written the main idea on one side of an index card and the details on the other side.	___	___
I have reviewed my index cards several times before taking the test.	___	___
I have used the association/visualization method to help me remember important information.	___	___
I have thought about the information the teacher is likely to ask on the test.	___	___
I have made up a practice test.	___	___
I think positive thoughts and repeat silent positive statements when studying	___	___

If you use all of the steps on this checklist when preparing for a test, you can pat yourself on the back. You have done first-rate job of studying, and your grades will improve.

What I Have Learned about Studying

Connect the statements with a line:

Taking notes	- powerful sentence that begins an essay
Turning title into a question	- helps you organize information
Turning subtitle into a question	- final sentence in an essay that ties everything together
Writing answers to questions	- method for remembering and understanding what you have read
Topic sentence	- helps you prepare for a test.
Seeing information in your mind	- helps you think about what the material is about
Concluding sentence	- helps you focus on the content you are studying
Thumb-nail outline	- helps you make up practice test questions
Thinking like a teacher	- a good way to study smart
Identifying main ideas and details	- helps you organize your essay
Making up practice tests	- reduces test anxiety
Thinking positive thoughts and silently reciting positive statements	- helps you memorize

In the next section of this book, you will learn powerful techniques for solving problems and for thinking and behaving more strategically.

Part 3

Thinking Smart

Unit 10

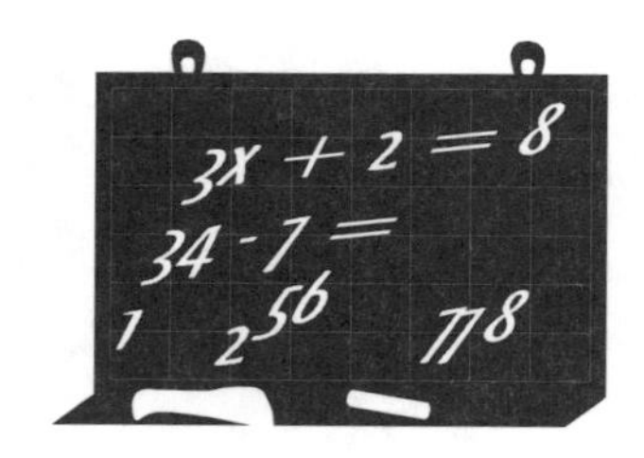

Problem-Solving

Surrounded by Chaos

Paul couldn't figure out why the door to his room wouldn't budge. He knew it wasn't locked from the inside. Putting his shoulder against the door, he pushed as hard as he could, but it only opened about two inches. Paul took three steps back, put both hands in front of him, and smashed into the door with all his strength. He heard a cracking sound, and the door finally opened enough for him to slip through. Once inside, he discovered that his football gear had fallen on the floor behind the door and was wedged against the leg of his desk. Paul was glad his mother hadn't seen him smash against the door, and he wondered if he had damaged the hinges.

Paul threw his book bag on his unmade bed and began to search through the piles of paper on his desk. He pushed aside the candy and chewing gum wrappers and the soft drink cans. He was looking for his science report that had been due today. He was certain the paper was somewhere in his room, but he had no idea where. When he couldn't find the report on his desk, he began to search under the piles of clean and dirty clothes on his bed. Finally, he found it under his dirty gym shorts. It was crumpled and creased, but it could still be read.

"If I hand it in tomorrow, maybe the teacher will still accept it," Paul thought to himself as he stuffed the report into his backpack.

As usual, Paul had put off writing the report until the last minute. He had received the assignment two weeks ago, but had waited until the night before it was due to start writing it. Of course, he hadn't had time to proofread the report. Then he had forgotten to take it to school.

Paul knew that his teacher would lower his grade because the assignment was late. Since most of his assignments were not handed in on time, he was accustomed to having his grades lowered. He was also accustomed to red marks all over his papers because of spelling and grammar errors.

Spelling had always been a nightmare for Paul. It seemed like the words were never spelled the way they sounded. The six years he had spent in the resource program helped, but he was still a terrible speller.

Paul's sloppy handwriting made things even worse. His papers were usually written on the school bus on the way to school, and each bump in the road caused a bump in his handwriting.

"So what!" Paul thought. "The teacher and my parents can get on my case all they want. I don't care! I can read my reports, and that's what counts."

Predicting What Will Happen

Go back to the story. Underline *one time* and number the specific behaviors that could cause Paul to be disorganized. (For example: piles of paper on his desk.) Then underline *two times* and number the specific attitudes that could affect his school performance.

Although you don't know Paul, you could probably make some reasonable predictions about his school performance. Indicate whether your predictions are *possible* or *probable.*

His grades in school:

1 2 3 4 5 6 7 8 9 10 ***Possible Probable***

Poor Average Excellent

His parents' attitudes about his attitude and effort:

1 2 3 4 5 6 7 8 9 10 ***Possible Probable***

Negative Average Positive

His teachers' attitudes about his attitude and effort:

1 2 3 4 5 6 7 8 9 10 ***Possible Probable***

Negative Average Positive

His likelihood of being a successful student:

1 2 3 4 5 6 7 8 9 10 ***Possible Probable***

Poor Average Excellent

The overall quality of his work:

1 2 3 4 5 6 7 8 9 10 ***Possible Probable***

Poor Average Excellent

His attitude about school:

1 2 3 4 5 6 7 8 9 10 ***Possible Probable***

Poor Average Excellent

His effort:

1 2 3 4 5 6 7 8 9 10 ***Possible Probable***

Poor Average Excellent

His chances of success in college:

1 2 3 4 5 6 7 8 9 10 ***Possible Probable***

Poor Average Excellent

DIBS: A Problem-Solving Method

As you read Paul's story, you probably concluded that he has "an attitude." You may have also concluded that unless he becomes more organized and changes his attitude, he's going to do poorly in school.

Let's say that Paul acknowledges that he has a problem and says that he would like to do better in school. Is there a way that Paul could solve his problem? The answer is "Yes!" Paul could use a powerful method that could help him solve the problem. The method, which is called **DIBS**, has four steps.

D = **<u>D</u>EFINE** the problem (say exactly what the problem is).

I = **<u>I</u>NVESTIGATE** what is causing the problem.

B = **<u>B</u>RAINSTORM** solutions to the problem (think up as many as possible).

S = **<u>S</u>ELECT** an idea to try out as a possible solution.

As you can see, the word **DIBS** is an acronym that is formed from the first letter of each step in the procedure. This acronym will help you remember the steps.

The first step of **DIBS--defining the problem**--can be tricky. You can easily get sidetracked and begin describing the *symptoms* of the problem instead of defining the actual problem. For example, you might be tempted to say that Paul's problem is that his room is a mess. Yes, it is true that his room is a mess, but this is *not* the problem. It is one of the *causes* or symptoms of the problem. This distinction will be clearer as you proceed.

Let's practice the **DIBS** method. To get you started, look at the possibilities listed below.

1. **<u>D</u>EFINE** Paul's problem (be specific).

   Paul ____

   ____

Choose the best definition from the following list and write it in the space above. Select the definition that best describes the entire problem and not just one symptom of the problem. *Although all of the following statements are true, one is a better overall definition of Paul's problem.*

- **Paul is disorganized.**
- **Paul is getting bad grades because he has a poor attitude and applies little effort in school.**
- **Paul leaves his work until the last minute**
- **Paul's report is sloppy because he wrote it on the bus.**

You can see that the second choice best describes Paul's problem. The other choices describe some of the specific factors that are causing or contributing to the overall problem. Write down the second choice in the space above.

Now let's look at the second step in the **DIBS** method. You are to indicate the causes of the problem. Four causes are listed on the previous page. Write those in the spaces below, and then see if you can find at least one more.

2. **INVESTIGATE** the causes of the problem. List as many reasons as you can that explain why Paul is doing poorly in school (Hint: You've underlined them already in the story. Summarize the most important reasons. For example, write down: *His room was a mess* instead of *He had dirty clothes on his bed* and *Candy wrappers on his desk.*)

   See if you can come up with *at least* five reasons.

   Reason # 1 ______________________________

   Reason # 2 ______________________________

   Reason # 3 ______________________________

   Reason # 4 ______________________________

   Reason # 5 ______________________________

   Reason # 6 ______________________________

3. **BRAINSTORM** solutions to the problem.

   1. ______________________________
   2. ______________________________
   3. ______________________________
   4. ______________________________
   5. ______________________________
   6. ______________________________

   Possible solutions:

   Budget enough time to complete homework assignments at home
   Organize his desk
   Ask a friend or parent to proofread his assignments and help find errors
   Create a study schedule
   Ask for help from the resource specialist if he is having difficulty writing reports
   Write reports on a computer and use spell-check to find errors

You can write these solutions in the spaces above, or you can brainstorm your own ideas. Try to brainstorm at least one additional solution on your own.

4. **S**ELECT the best idea from the list that could help Paul solve the problem.

____

____

Was the idea you selected specific enough to help Paul? For example, if you wrote *Be more organized* or *Improve his attitude*, do you think Paul would have an easy time figuring out how to do that? Examples of more specific suggestions might include *Put papers into files for each subject*, or *Make up a schedule for doing schoolwork.*

Practicing the DIBS Method

Use the **DIBS** system to find solutions to the following problems. Remember the steps:

D = **D**EFINE the problem (say exactly what the problem is).

I = **I**NVESTIGATE what is causing the problem.

B = **B**RAINSTORM solutions to the problem (think up as many as possible).

S = **S**ELECT an idea to try out as a possible solution.

1. You are having difficulty understanding the information in your science textbook. You often study the wrong material, and you have trouble recalling important facts. You think there's a good chance that you will fail the next test.

   D: ____

   I: ____

   ____

   ____

   ____

   B: ____

   ____

   S: ____

How DIBS Can Be Used to Solve This Problem

Define: I will probably fail the next science test

Investigate: I am having difficulty understanding the information in my textbook.

I don't know what to study.

I don't know how to prepare for the tests.

I cannot remember the important information.

Brainstorm: I could ask my parents to help me study for the test.

I could ask the teacher for extra help.

I could ask my resource specialist for help.

I could study with a friend who is doing well in the course.

Select: I'll ask my resource specialist to help me prepare for the test.*

*** Your DIBS "answers" may be different than these, and they may still be perfectly acceptable.**

2. You are spending five hours every night doing homework, and you are usually working until 10:30 every evening. This often causes you to fall asleep in class.

D: ______________________________

I: ______________________________

____

____

____

B: ______________________________

____

S: ______________________________

3. Your friends want you to go to the movies with them on Saturday, but your parents have given you a list of chores to do.

D: ______________________________

I: ____

____

____

____

B: ____

____

S: ____

4. Your soccer coach believes you are not hustling during practice and has benched you.

D: ____

I: ____

____

____

____

B: ____

____

S: ____

Mastery: Further Practice with DIBS

Here are some more problems you can solve using **DIBS**. Use a separate piece of paper.

Problem # 1: A kid in school is telling your friends that you cheated on a test. You didn't cheat.

Problem # 2: The teacher announces that there will be an important test tomorrow. You have made plans with your parents to go shopping at the mall for new clothes.

Problem # 3: You have been sick for a week and have fallen behind, especially in math. You're confused about the work, and you feel that you will never be able to catch up.

Problem # 4: Your two best friends are in trouble with their parents. They ask you to tell their parents something that isn't true so that they won't be grounded for the weekend.

Problem # 5: You see a friend stealing from another student's backpack

Problem # 6: Your younger sister tells your parents that you're teasing her. Each time she tells on you, you get in trouble.

Problem # 7: Your parents accuse you of being lazy and irresponsible. They complain that you are not doing your chores, and they threaten to take away certain privileges.

What I Have Learned about Solving Problems

	True	False
Before you can solve a problem, you need to define the problem accurately.	____	____
Defining a problem accurately doesn't require much thought or effort.	____	____
The more specific the description of the problem, the easier it is to investigate the causes, brainstorm solutions, and solve the problem.	____	____
Brainstorming is letting your mind think of as many ideas as possible and may include ideas that might appear unimportant or silly.	____	____
Specific solutions are less useful than general solutions.	____	____
To solve a problem, you don't need to know what is causing the problem.	____	____
You can make predictions about what is likely to happen based on a person's behavior and attitudes.	____	____
Most problems can be solved if you learn an effective problem-solving system.	____	____

Unit 11

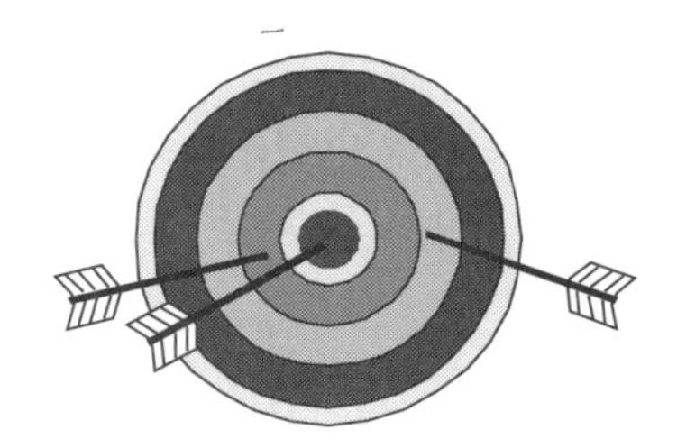

Goals

Figuring Out How to Get What You Want

As usual, Brittany was shooting baskets when her father got home from work at 6:15. Her dad pulled the car into the driveway, got out, and watched her take lay-ups and shoot jump shots. Smiling at him, she waved hello. She then began to shoot baskets from the white foul line that she had painted on the driveway.

"Nice arc, honey. Those are sweet swish shots. No rim," her dad commented.

"Thanks," Brittany yelled without losing her concentration.

"Big improvement."

Brittany smiled again. She valued her dad's opinion. He had played four years of college basketball at UCLA, and he had coached her team when she was in elementary school. He was also very honest when he evaluated her playing. If she were doing something wrong, he would tell her. When he said she was doing something right, she believed him. His approval meant a lot to her.

"Let's go in. I'm sure Mom has dinner ready."

Brittany passed him the ball and he sunk it from twenty feet. The ball didn't hit the rim.

Within five minutes, they were all seated at the kitchen table. Brittany loaded her plate with a chicken breast and mashed potatoes. Her little brother passed her the peas. "How was practice?" her father asked.

"Terrible. The coach is always pushing me. I may not make the varsity."

"What's the problem?"

"The coach says I'm not trying hard enough. But I am trying! I realize that I am not consistent. Some days I play well, and other days I don't play well. The coach has said my shooting is OK, but she's not happy with the way I pass the ball and play defense. Dad, I work very hard in practice. I don't know what I can do to get better. I think the coach is just being unfair."

"And why is that?" her father asked.

"She just doesn't like me."

"Could it be that she's hard on you because she thinks you are capable of playing better?" he asked calmly.

Brittany didn't answer right away. She stared at the table and seemed lost in thought.

"Maybe," she finally responded sadly.

"Do you want to be on the varsity, Brittany?"

"Of course I do! I'll feel horrible if I have to do another year of j.v. I know I'm only a freshman, but lots of freshman make the varsity their sophomore year."

"Do you have any ideas about how you could improve your game?"

"No. Maybe I'm not as good as you think I am."

"Have you spoken to the coach about the problem?"

"Yes. All she says is that I'm not working hard enough."

"And that's not true, right?"

"It's not true."

"Do you see any solutions?"

"Work harder, I guess."

"Has she told you what you need to work on?"

"My passes and my defense."

"Do you think the coach would be willing to spend some extra time helping you?"

"Yes."

"Perhaps it would be a good idea to tell her that you would like some help. Maybe you could talk to her tomorrow."

"OK."

"When could you work with the coach?"

"I guess I could suit up quickly and get to practice 10 minutes early."

"That seems like a good idea. Any other ideas?"

"I can't think of any."

"How about a personal training program?"

"What do you mean?"

"You said you needed to improve your passing and your defense. The next step is to figure out a method to improve these skills. How could you do this?"

"I could talk to the coach and ask for suggestions."

"Good thinking. Is there anything else you could do?" her father asked.

"I could work with you at home after practice and on the weekends. I could also arrange some pickup games with some of the girls on the j.v. squad and the varsity. We could play at the park or maybe one of the school playgrounds."

"Sounds like a good idea to me. You could develop your own training program. If you want, I could also work with you. Perhaps your dad can still show you a thing or two about passing and defense."

"That would be great!"

"We can start tomorrow. I'll try to get home early, and we can maybe get a half-hour in before dinner. I'll also set an hour aside to work with you on Saturday mornings. You try to arrange a game on Saturday afternoon, and I'll come over to the park and give you guys some pointers. Sound OK?"

"Thanks, Dad. I know the girls would be really excited about having you coach them."

"There's one important condition attached to this proposal. You can't let your studying slide. Academics are still the number-one priority in this family. You'll have to budget your time carefully so that you can keep to your study schedule. The extra time that you're going to spend on basketball will have to be taken from your free time and not from your study time. Agreed?"

"Agreed."

"After dinner, let's put together a personal training program that will help you to improve your game. The first step is for you to write down your long-term goals and short-term goals. You need to be very specific. How does that sound?"

"Good."

Brittany no longer felt discouraged. She was certain that with her coach's help and her dad's help, she would figure how to improve her skills and make the varsity.

Brittany's Goal Chart

Long-Term Goals:

- Make the varsity basketball team.
- Score a minimum of ten points each game next year on the varsity squad.
- Impress the varsity coach with my effort and abilities.
- Earn a basketball scholarship at a first-rate college.

Short-Term Goals:

- Ask for extra help from my coach.
- Spend an extra 25 minutes each day after practice improving my technique.
- Ask my coach to evaluate my work, effort, and improvement each week.
- Score a minimum of eight points each game.

Checking Out Feelings

Brittany had a problem and was frustrated and discouraged. At first, she was upset with her coach. Why? ______________________________

____

Later in the story, she also seemed to be upset with herself? Why? ______________________________

____

Brittany's father helped her come up with a plan to solve the problem. What effect did this have? ______________________________

____

____

Why did the plan produce this effect? ______________________________

____

How would you rate the way Brittany's dad handled the situation?

1 2 3 4 5 6 7 8 9 10

Poor Average Excellent

Why? ____

____

Solving Problems

As Brittany and her father discussed the situation, Brittany realized she could probably solve her problem. Go back and underline and number each idea or solution that she and her dad came up with. You should be able to find at least seven ideas.

Do you think the problem-solving ideas Brittany and her dad brainstormed were smart? How would you rate their plan?

1 2 3 4 5 6 7 8 9 10

Not Smart Fairly Smart Very Smart

List any other ideas you can think of that might help Brittany resolve her problem.

1. ____
2. ____
3. ____
4. ____
5. ____

What Are Your Goals?

You have probably thought about what you might want to do after you finish school. Perhaps you plan on going to college. Perhaps you dream about becoming a professional basketball player, firefighter, musician, engineer, veterinarian, or attorney. If you do have such goals, these would be considered long-range career goals.

Some kids know at a very early age what they want to do with their lives, and they never alter their course. A student with exceptional musical talent may know when she is six that she wants to be a concert pianist. Another student whose mom is a physician may decide in third grade that he too wants to be a doctor, and he may plan his life around going to medical school.

He will focus on taking science and math classes in high school and college, and because getting into medical school is very difficult, he will strive to get the best grades he can.

For most people, however, their goals are likely to change many times during their lives. An eighth grader who decides that she wants to become a lawyer may decide in high school that she really wants to become an actress. A ninth grader who wants to become a police officer may decide later that he wants to become an accountant.

Even though your goals may change, having personal goals is still important. Goals motivate you to become the best you can be. They provide a sense of direction and purpose. They inspire you to make the required effort, and they help you focus on what is most important to you.

The Function of Goals

Provide focus

Encourage motivation

Inspire effort

Provide a sense of direction and purpose

Encourage commitment

Stimulate achievement

Generate pride

Build self-confidence

The gymnast who wants to win an Olympics gold medal must make an absolute commitment to training, and she must continuously focus her emotional and physical energy on attaining her goal. She must be willing spend her free time at the gym, and she must be willing to make significant sacrifices. If she is a really serious competitor, she may have to get up at 5:00 AM and work with her coach before school. Her weekends and after-school time would be dedicated to practicing. The same need for discipline and focus applies in the case of the student who wants to become a concert violinist or an astronaut.

Even though your personal goals may be less demanding, you should be willing to stretch for the achievements that are important to you. You must also be willing to devote the necessary time and effort to get what you want. Your immediate goal may be a good grade on the next math test or two hits in the next baseball game. Your long-term goal may be to make the varsity baseball team in tenth grade or earn a scholarship to college.

Kids who have goals are like guided missiles. They may not hit the target every time, but they do more often than not. When they do attain their objectives, they feel accomplished, proud, and powerful. Each success builds their self-confidence.

Achieving what you set out to achieve is like starting to eat an ice cream sundae. It tastes so good that once you start, you don't want to stop.

If you currently have goals, list them below. If you don't have any right now, make some up. Don't worry! You can always change them later.

MY PERSONAL GOALS

Date: _______

1. ______________________________
2. ______________________________
3. ______________________________
4. ______________________________
5. ______________________________

You may have listed goals you want to achieve when you become an adult. For example, your goal may be a teacher, a lawyer, a dancer, or a veterinarian. Or you may have written "go to college" or "make a lot of money." These are **LONG-TERM GOALS** that you must work hard to achieve in the future. If your long-term goal is to become a professional hockey player, you would need to be aware that the competition is going to be incredibly stiff, as there are relatively few professional hockey players in the world. To have a chance at attaining this goal, you would need to play extraordinarily well in high school and college, and you would need superior endorsements from your coaches about your skills, desire, effort, and commitment. If you are exceptionally talented and highly motivated, you may get drafted, and a professional team might offer you a multi-million dollar contract.

Let's assume you wrote down that you want to be the best basketball player on your team. This could be a long-term goal, especially if you feel it will take some time before you become the best player. If you wrote down "score at least fifteen points in the next game," this would be a **SHORT-TERM GOAL** because it's something you want to achieve right away. Another example of a **short-term goal** would be to get a B on your next book report. Your **long-term goal** might be to get a B in science on your next report card. An even-longer-term goal would be to get a degree in engineering and work for an electronics firm. Obviously, there is value in having both types of goals.

Review the goals that you wrote down and separate them into **long-term** and **short-term goals.** Feel free to add to the list if you wish.

MY LONG-TERM GOALS

1. ______________________________
2. ______________________________
3. ______________________________
4. ______________________________
5. ______________________________

MY SHORT-TERM GOALS

1. ______________________________
2. ______________________________
3. ______________________________
4. ______________________________
5. ______________________________

When you decide on a goal and then figure out a plan for achieving it, you've created a **STRATEGY**. We'll examine strategies for attaining your goals in another unit.

Let's review what you have learned so far:

List as many reasons as you can for having goals:

1. ______________________________
2. ______________________________
3. ______________________________
4. ______________________________
5. ______________________________
6. ______________________________

A Letter to Myself -- My Goals in School

Now that you understand the reason for having goals, do the following activity for fun. You can copy the short- and long-term goals you have already written down.

Date: ____________________

My Name: ____________________________________

My Address: ____________________________________

____

Dear Me:

I'm writing this letter to myself to record my current **Long-Term Goals** and **Short-Term Academic Goals**. I understand that I can change my goals later, but I agree not to change my long-term and short-term goals for the next three months. I will tape this letter near my desk or on the wall near my bed. I will periodically review my short-term goals to remind myself of my objectives and to make certain that I am doing all that I can to attain the grades I have targeted.

LONG-TERM GOALS

1. ____
2. ____
3. ____
4. ____

SPECIFIC SHORT-TERM ACADEMIC GOALS

Subject	Most Recent Report Card Grades	Grade I Want on Next Report Card
Math	__________	__________
__________	__________	__________
__________	__________	__________
__________	__________	__________
__________	__________	__________
__________	__________	__________

Yours truly,

____

An Experiment with Goal-Setting

As you have learned, personal goals can be a powerful motivator. In fact, most successful people continually establish and reestablish goals. When they achieve a particular objective, they congratulate themselves, and then they establish a new objective to replace the one they have attained. The runner who wants to run a marathon may have a short-term goal to be able to run five miles. When she achieves this interim goal, her next interim goal may be to run seven miles. After each interim goal is fulfilled, she methodically establishes a new one. The short-term or interim goals are thus stepping-stones that lead to the ultimate objective of being able to run a twenty-six-mile marathon.

During the next two weeks, make a point of writing down a weekly goal on Monday morning. In this experiment, focus exclusively on establishing a specific academic goal such as a B on the next weekly math test or science quiz. Then write down a short-term goal for every day of the week. At the end of the day, check "yes" or "no" to indicate whether or not you have attained your daily goal. On Friday, check "yes" or "no" to indicate whether or not you have attained your weekly goal.

Week #1		**YES**	**NO**
Weekly Goal:	______________________________	___	___
Daily Goals:			
Mon.:	______________________________	___	___
Tues.:	______________________________	___	___
Wed.:	______________________________	___	___
Thurs.:	______________________________	___	___
Fri.:	______________________________	___	___

Week #2		**YES**	**NO**
Weekly Goal:	______________________________	___	___
Daily Goals:			
Mon.:	______________________________	___	___
Tues.:	______________________________	___	___
Wed.:	______________________________	___	___
Thurs.:	______________________________	___	___
Fri.:	______________________________	___	___

If you're pleased with the results of the experiment, continue writing down your daily and weekly goals for the rest of the school year. You will probably discover that your work and grades will improve dramatically. You will be proud of your accomplishments, and your parents and teachers will be delighted with your progress.

Using Goals To Solve Problems

In Unit 10, you learned how to use **DIBS** to solve problems. Establishing goals can be another powerful problem-solving tool. Why learn another method? Well, do you recall when you learned the **"Chewing-Up Information" Method**? You had already learned how to mind-map, and you may have thought that you didn't need to learn another study method. What you discovered was that mind-mapping method may be a more effective study technique in certain situations, and the **"Chewing-Up Information" Method** may be more effective in other situations. You may have also discovered that in certain situations, it is smart to combine both study methods. The same principle applies to problem-solving. **DIBS** may work best when solving certain problems, and the **4-Part Goal-Setting System** that you are about to learn may work best with other types of problems. Knowing more than one way to do something gives you more choices. Like a golfer, you can look in your bag and select the best club for each situation. In the following story, a student is confronted with a problem. The goal-setting method is then used to solve the problem.

Situation: Roberto wanted to go on a camping trip to Yellowstone Park with his best friend during spring break. His friend's family was planning on spending seven days at the park, and they agreed to take Roberto with them. Roberto's parents, however, were angry at him because his grades had slipped, and they told him that he couldn't go. They insisted that he spend the spring break studying. Roberto was very upset. He wanted to persuade his parents to change their mind. Spring break was in six weeks. How could Roberto get his parents to relent and allow him to go camping with his friend?

4-Part Goal-Setting System for Solving Problems

Step 1: Define the challenge.

Step 2: Define a goal that could allow you to overcome the challenge.

Step 3: Establish practical short-term goals.

Step 4: List specific actions that would allow you to attain short-term and long-term goals.

Let's see how the **4-Part Goal-Setting System** could be used to solve Roberto's problem.

Challenge: Convince my parents that I should be allowed to go on camping trip and change their attitude about my schoolwork.

Goal: Improve my school performance during the next 6 weeks.

Short-term Goals:

1. Do my homework without having to be reminded.
2. Complete all my assignments.
3. Improve my grades on homework assignments, tests, and reports.
4. Study very hard.

Specifics:

1. Carefully record my assignments.
2. Check off each completed assignment on my assignment sheet.
3. Maintain a study schedule.
4. Use mind-mapping, note-taking, and test-review methods.
5. After improving my school performance for 4 weeks, ask my parents to reconsider their decision and allow me to go on the camping trip.

Using the preceding procedure as a model and use the **4-Part Goal-Setting System** to solve the following problems.

1. You want to persuade your mom to allow you to go to a party on Saturday night. Your mom is mad at you because you have been teasing your kid brother, and she says you can't go to the party.

2. You need a B in your science course to qualify for a college scholarship. There are four weeks left in the semester, and you are currently carry a C in the class.

3. You want to persuade your baseball coach to let you play on the varsity. The junior-varsity coach thinks you're not working hard during practice.

4. You need extra money to go with your friends to a concert. Your parents have given you the permission to go, but they won't give you the money for the ticket because they feel you've spent money on things that they consider wasteful.

Challenge: ______________________________

____

Goal: ______________________________

____

Short-Term Goals: ______________________________

____

____

____

Specifics: ______________________________

____

____

____

Challenge:

Goal:

Short-Term Goals:

Specifics:

Challenge:

Goal:

Short-Term Goals:

Specifics:

Challenge: ______________________________

____

Goal: ______________________________

____

Short-Term Goals: ______________________________

____

____

____

Specifics: ______________________________

____

____

____

What I Have Learned about Goals

(Draw a line from the word to the correct definition)

Goals	Something you want in the far future
Short-term goals	Feelings produced by getting what you want
Long-term goals	Behaviors that allow you to achieve what you want
Motivation and effort	An objective you want to achieve
Commitment, dedication, and effort	Something you want in the near future
Goal-setting	Behavior that is triggered when you have goals
Pride, power, and self-confidence	A powerful means for solving problem

Unit 12

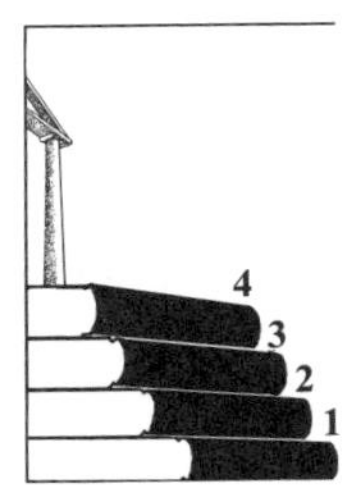

Priorities

Figuring Out the Right Order

When the class completed their work early, the math teacher would usually give the students a "brain teaser" to solve during the remaining few minutes. If they couldn't finish solving the problem in class, they would be expected to do it for homework. The problems were always interesting, and Rasheed looked forward to solving them.

Rasheed was especially intrigued by the problem his teacher posed on Friday. She told the students that because of a series of awful blizzards, a remote Eskimo village had radioed that they urgently needed food and medical supplies to get through the next three months of winter. Unless they received immediate help, many of the one hundred inhabitants in the village would perish. The village was located over 600 miles from the nearest town, and the supply plane would have to fly over long stretches of barren frozen tundra. During winter, the temperature on the ground was 10 degrees below zero.

The teacher explained that there would be only one opportunity to re-supply the village before winter storms and darkness would make landing a plane on the deep, swirling snow impossible. The assignment was to decide what supplies to pack on the plane.

Each student was told to make up a list of materials that would be essential to the survival of the villagers. Because of fuel requirements and space limitations, the total weight of the supplies could not exceed 750 pounds. If the supplies weighed more, the pilot would not be able to carry enough fuel to make it back to the airport.

The teacher instructed the class to figure out what to pack on the plane. The challenge was to provide sufficient vital supplies that did not exceed the maximum weight requirement. The teacher informed the class that they could begin working on the problem during the last fifteen minutes of class. Their homework over the weekend would be to finish working on the assignment. They were to bring their list of supplies to class on Monday. The assignment would be for extra credit, and they would be graded on the quality of the list they created and their ability to stay within the weight limits.

Rasheed found the problem fascinating, and he immediately began to think about what supplies to include. He began writing down ideas in class. When the bell rang, he was still writing. On Saturday after much thought, he began to make up an actual list of the items he felt were essential for the survival of inhabitants of the village. He decided to allocate 50 pounds for medical supplies, and 100 pounds for heating oil. As he began to consider what specific food to pack on the plane, he used his own preferences as a guide. Below is his list:

ITEM	**WEIGHT** (in pounds)
Dry ice for refrigerating fresh food during transit	20
Medical supplies	50
Heating oil	100
Milk	50
Meat	100
Fish	100
Cereal	25
Fresh vegetables	25
Canned fruit	30
Frozen fruit	25
Cheese	50
Pasta and pasta sauce	50
Frozen pizza	50
Frozen bread	50
Frozen vegetables	35
Condensed soup	50
Hot dogs and bologna	50

Mustard and relish	10
Potato chips	20
Ice cream	50
Candy	50
Frozen pies	50
Popcorn	15
Canned and frozen juice	50

Rasheed felt that he had included all the supplies that the villagers would need, but when he added up the weight of the items, he discovered the supplies exceeded the weight limit by three hundred and thirty-five pounds! He decided he would need to eliminate some items and reduce the weight of other items.

He realized that he could reduce the weight by carrying 50% less candy, frozen pies, and potato chips. He could also lower the weight by reducing the quantity of many of the items and by eliminating the less-essential supplies. For example, he decided the villagers could get by without popcorn, but even with these adjustments, his list was still way over the weight limit.

Aware that he had to revise his list, Rasheed decided to discuss the problem with his dad. He recommended that Rasheed place the most important gear at the top of the page and list the less essential items below it in order of their importance. His father explained this process was called "establishing priorities." He suggested that Rasheed begin by numbering his original list in order of importance to survival. To help, he wrote down three steps for establishing priorities.

Steps for Establishing Priorities

1. Write down items most essential to survival.
2. Number the list in order of importance. (The most essential items should be at the top).
3. If necessary, eliminate items at the bottom of the list that are less essential.

Rasheed recognized that meat, fish, heating fuel, medical supplies, vegetables, and fruit would have to be at the top of the list because these items were the most essential to survival. Having frozen pies would be nice, but they were certainly not essential to survival and had a lower priority. He also realized that he could use powdered milk, powdered soup, powdered juice, and freeze-dried vegetables, and, in so doing, significantly reduce the weight of these items and the weight of the dry ice he would have to carry. Once Rasheed listed the materials in order of priority, he could decide what to eliminate and how to reduce the weight of specific supplies.

It was hard work making decisions about priorities and weight limits. After some strategic thinking, Rasheed put together an excellent survival package that met the weight requirements. The math teacher told him he had done a great job and gave him an A on the assignment.

Learning How to Establish Priorities

Imagine you had to solve the same problem. Reorganize Rasheed's list, placing the most important items for survival at the top of the list. Follow these steps:

1. **Cross off non-essential items.**
2. **Number Rasheed's original list in order of importance to survival.** (For example, you might put: #1 meat or fish; #2 heating oil; and #3 medical supplies.)
3. **Whenever possible, reduce weight of items on the list.**

Figure out a way to reduce the total weight of the supplies to 750 pounds. When you are finished making adjustments, add up the weight of all the items on the new list. If you have met the weight requirements, rewrite the list below. If you have not, make additional changes. Remember to prioritize your list and to place the items in the order of their importance to survival.

Revised List of Supplies

	Item	Weight		Item	Weight
1.	________	____	11.	________	____
2.	________	____	12.	________	____
3.	________	____	13.	________	____
4.	________	____	14.	________	____
5.	________	____	15.	________	____
6.	________	____	16.	________	____
7.	________	____	17.	________	____
8.	________	____	18	________	____
9.	________	____	19.	________	____
10	________	____	20.	________	____

Now list the items you eliminated, and briefly tell why. Write *"not necessary," "not practical,"* or *"not important"* after the item.

	Item Eliminated	**Reason**
1.	____________________	____________________
2.	____________________	____________________
3.	____________________	____________________
4.	____________________	____________________
5.	____________________	____________________
6.	____________________	____________________
7	.____________________	____________________

How would you rate the emergency supply "package" you put together?

1 2 3 4 5 6 7 8 9 10

Poor Fair Excellent

Establishing Your Own Priorities

Projects and challenges become more manageable when you establish priorities and list things in order of importance or necessity. This process may be referred to as establishing a hierarchy. The procedure can be applied to establishing your long-term and short-term goals. For example, you may have a list of short-term or interim goals that you believe will allow you to attain your long-term goal. By prioritizing the steps, you can determine a logical and practical order for completing them. Then you can create a schedule and check off each completed task or interim step. Your priority list will help you become organized and work more efficiently.

Let's say that your history teacher announces that a term paper is due in three weeks and that the paper has to be a minimum of fifteen pages. She lists ten topics, and instructs students to select a topic from the list. To get started, you could list the required steps to complete the assignment and then list them in the order of priority. This process of establishing priorities will keep you from becoming overwhelmed and feeling that there are too many things to do and too little time to do them.

For practice, let's prioritize the tasks that need to be completed to write a history term paper. The required steps are listed below. Prioritize the steps in the order in which the steps should be done. Start with the tasks you need to do first. Number the list in order of priority.

Writing a History Term Paper

12 Write the final draft.

2 Go to the library.

5 Go on-line and see if you can find relevant information.

10 Check for spelling and grammar mistakes.

3 Check out the necessary books.

7 Write notes on index cards.

1 Choose a topic.

6 Write down quotations.

11 Make up a bibliography.

13 Turn in the report on time.

4 Read material about the subject in the encyclopedia, using either the actual volumes or CD software.

9 Write first draft.

8 Put index cards in order.

There is a certain amount of flexibility in prioritizing this list. Some students may prefer to make up their bibliography *after* writing their final draft. Others may prefer to do this step *before* writing the final draft. Both procedures are perfectly acceptable. What's important is that you think carefully about a logical order for doing the steps that will allow you to complete the assignment efficiently.

Combining Priorities and Goals

Review your list of personal **SHORT-TERM GOALS** on page 158. These are the interim steps that will allow you to attain your **LONG-TERM GOALS.** By targeting the short-term goals in the proper sequence, you significantly improve the likelihood of being able to attain your long-term goal.

If you feel that a particular short-term goal is more important or has priority over another short-term goal, re-number the order of your list of short-term goals. If the original order still seems correct, you do not need to re-number your list.

Mastery: More Practice Establishing Priorities

Imagine you and your family want to do some cross-country skiing during winter break. Your parents decide to rent a cabin in an isolated area in Colorado. You have snow tires on the four-wheel-drive SUV, and you have chains, but your father is concerned that you might become stranded if there is a severe snow storm or a blizzard. He wants you to make certain that you pack enough survival gear in the car to survive in a worst-case situation.

He asks you to make up a list of emergency supplies that need to be packed. You think of everything that you might possibly need, and you write down the following list:

Flashlights
Warm blankets
Warm clothes
Walkman & CDs
Bottled water
Cell phone
Emergency signaling tarp
Canned heat canisters
Snow shoes
Powered soup
Matches and cigarette lighter
Freeze-dried food
Portable grill
School books
First-aid kit
Candy
Briquettes
Extra batteries
Battery-powered radio
Maps and compass
Games
Flares
Sleeping bags
Tent

When you show the list to your dad, he tells you there isn't enough room for all of these supplies and that you will have to eliminate non-essential and less-essential items. Make a priority list of the items on the list. Place the most important things at top. There are twenty-four items in the original list. The final list should have no more than sixteen items.

1. ____________________ 2. ____________________
3. ____________________ 4. ____________________
5. ____________________ 6. ____________________
7. ____________________ 8. ____________________
9. ____________________ 10. ____________________
11. ____________________ 12 ____________________
13. ____________________ 14. ____________________
15. ____________________ 16. ____________________

Now list the eight items you eliminated and tell why you eliminated them.

Items Eliminated	Reason
1. ____________	____________
2. ____________	____________
3. ____________	____________
4. ____________	____________
5. ____________	____________
6. ____________	____________
7. ____________	____________
8. ____________	____________

How would you rate the emergency supply "package" you put together?

1 2 3 4 5 6 7 8 9 10

Poor **Fair** **Excellent**

Applying Priorities in Your Life

Now that you know how to establish priorities, you can use this skill in many areas of your life. For example, you could list what you would like to take with you on a camping trip (food, sleeping bag, flashlight, lantern, tent, soft drinks, water, fishing rods, warm clothes, compass, ice chest, etc.) and then prioritize the list. This can be helpful if you conclude that you cannot carry everything you want in the car. You could use your priority list to eliminate some less-important items. You could use the same prioritizing procedure when packing for a vacation (toothbrush, clean clothes, games, etc.) Once you get in the habit of automatically establishing your priorities, the procedure will become easy. Before long, you'll be setting priorities without even having to think about it.

A Plan That Didn't Work

On page 173, you did an activity in which you prepared a list of emergency supplies to take on a cross-country skiing vacation. Pretend that a student named Raul is actually asked by his father to make up a list of emergency supplies prior to a ski vacation. He prioritizes the list and eliminates eight items. His father approves of his "emergency package" and asks Raul to load the car with all of the supplies and gear they are planning to take to the ski cabin.

Raul begins to load the car. First he puts in an ice chest with the soft drinks, food, fresh fruit, snacks, and water. He then puts the emergency road flares in the trunk. After packing these items, he puts in the tarp, maps, compass, radio, batteries, cell phone, sleeping bags, snowshoes, first-aid kit, freeze-dried food, matches, canned-heat canisters, blankets, candy, and extra warm clothes. Just as he is about to pack the suitcases and fasten the skis on the top of the car, Raul's dad comes out of the house, takes a look at what is packed in the trunk, and tells Raul that he has not loaded the car properly.

Why do you think Raul's dad told him that he was packing the trunk of the car improperly?

____

____

____

What items might the family want to have *during* the car trip to the park? ________________

____

____

____

Where would you put the items you would need *during* the trip? _______________________

____

____

____

Where would you put the items you would want when you get to the ski cabin?

____

____

Look carefully at the **complete** list of gear Raul's family was planning to take to the cabin. The list includes the emergency supplies, which logically should be put in <u>after</u>, the ski clothes but <u>before</u> the ice chest. Make a priority list for loading the trunk. Number each item in the order in which you would place it in the trunk. #1 would be the item that you would put in first. This would be placed in the rear of the trunk, and it would be something that you wouldn't need until you arrived at the cabin. The highest numbers on your list would be put into the trunk last. These are items you would want to be able to get quickly. (Please note: You would obviously want to place all perishables such as food and milk inside the ice chest. Certain snacks and soft drinks would also go inside the ice chest.)

Lantern
Folding table
Charcoal lighter
Emergency food
Snacks for trip
Snowshoes
Canned-heat canisters
Walkman
Blankets
Tape player
Flashlights
Portable radio
First-aid Kit
Ski goggles
Food

Ski clothes
Charcoal
Water
Hatchet
Condiments
Travelers' checks
Ice chest
Fresh fruit
Condiments
Briquettes
Cooking utensils
Emergency tarp
Extra warm clothes
Walkie-talkies
Soft drinks

Sleeping bags
Napkins
Extra batteries
Soft drinks
Clothes
Books
Emergency flares
Compass
Matches and lighter
Hiking boots
Sleeping bags
Cell phone
Skis
Laptop computer
Fruit juice

CDs
Maps
Suitcases
Games
Towels
Grill
Cell phone
Pots
Candy
Soap
Blankets
Knife
Coffee
Milk
Shampoo

What I Have Learned about Priorities

TRUE/FALSE

_______ It is easier to get started on a project when you write down all the steps.

_______ Only adults need to worry about establishing priorities.

_______ Establishing priorities makes jobs more manageable.

_______ It is dumb to waste extra time establishing priorities.

_______ Always put the difficult things off until last.

_______ Always do things in the order that makes the most sense.

_______ It can sometimes be difficult figuring out what's most important or essential.

_______ Figuring out what's most important makes organization easier.

_______ Thinking about projects before you do them wastes valuable time.

_______ You don't need to think about establishing priorities until you are in college.

_______ Establishing priorities can help you achieve a goal.

_______ The procedure of establishing priorities is only important when doing schoolwork.

_______ When establishing priorities, you always have to write down your list on paper.

_______ Sometimes you can establish priorities in your head and don't need to make a written list of things to do.

Unit 13

Strategies

Getting What You Want

Courtney fell in love with acting when she was three-years-old. For as long as she could remember, she and her older sister Stephanie would entertain the family with little skits every evening after dinner. Their nine-year-old brother Conner would use reading lamps as spotlights and would point them at the makeshift stage that was located in front of the living room fireplace.

Courtney's parents and any neighbors or relatives they could corral would be seated in a row of folding chair in front of this makeshift stage. Conner would handle the lighting from a table behind the spectators. The lamps were placed on shaky piles of books, and Conner would point them at whoever was speaking or singing. Sometimes he would have to scurry from the lighting table to the stage because he usually had a part in most of the skits.

Stephanie, who was ten-years-old, would write, direct, and act in the productions, and there were always several cameo appearances for her little sister. Courtney loved to be the center of attention, and she would often upstage her brother and sister. They did not particularly appreciate this, but they couldn't help laughing at Courtney's antics. She was cute and outgoing and loved to sing and act funny. She also loved the applause.

Courtney decided in elementary school that she would be a professional actress when she grew up. When she watched TV or went to a movie, she was more concerned with the acting than she was with the plot. She would pay careful attention to the actor's facial expressions and movements. She and Stephanie would discuss and critique their performance. Every year their parents would permit them to stay up late to watch the Academy Awards and the Emmys.

One of the friends of Courtney's parents was a part-time actor, and when he came to visit, Courtney loved to talk with him about acting. She told Seth about her desire to become an actress and asked him how to develop a plan that would allow her to achieve her goal. Seth gave her lots of information about how to get started, and he described in detail the steps along the way. He also suggested that she read some biographies about famous actors and actresses. He told her that this might give her ideas about how to launch her career.

Courtney's older sister was now a senior in high school. Having decided that she wanted to write plays and direct, Stephanie was planning to attend a university with an excellent drama department. One day Stephanie took Courtney to meet her high school drama teacher. The teacher was very supportive and gave Courtney excellent suggestions and advice. With the information provided by the drama teacher and Seth, and with Stephanie's help, Courtney developed the following career strategy.

A Strategy for Becoming an Actress

1. Try out for every play in elementary, middle, and high school.
2. Try out for every play put on in the community that has parts for children.
3. Take private singing, acting, and dancing classes.
4. Get good grades in school.
2. Go to a good college with an excellent drama department.
3. Major in acting.
4. Get good grades in college.
5. After graduation, take classes in acting at a professional acting school.
6. Try out for local theater productions and for TV productions.
7. Move to New York or Los Angeles.
8. Find a theatrical agent.

Courtney looked at her plan and thought: "This won't be so difficult. If I work hard, I know I can do it."

Courtney felt good about her plan. Now that she knew what she needed to do to achieve her goal, she was certain she would succeed.

Taking a Close Look at Someone Else's Strategy

How would you evaluate Courtney's procedure for getting information about how to launch an acting career?

1 2 3 4 5 6 7 8 9 10

Not Smart Fairly Smart Very Smart

How would you evaluate her strategy for achieving her goal?

1 2 3 4 5 6 7 8 9 10

Not Smart Fairly Smart Very Smart

Look at the eight goals in Courtney's strategy and separate them into short- and long-term goals.

Courtney's Short-Term Goals

1. ______________________________
2. ______________________________
3. ______________________________
4. ______________________________

Courtney's Long-Term Goals

1. ______________________________
2. ______________________________
3. ______________________________
4. ______________________________

If Courtney follows her strategy, how likely do you think it is that she will attain her long-term goal and become an actress.

1 2 3 4 5 6 7 8 9 10

Unlikely Somewhat Likely Very Likely

Why? ______________________________

____

____

Although it wasn't mentioned in the story, list possible problems or challenges Courtney might encounter on the road to becoming a professional actress.

1. ______________________________
2. ______________________________
3. ______________________________
4. ______________________________
5. ______________________________

Developing an Effective Strategy

When you develop an effective strategy, there are six very important questions you need to ask yourself before you begin:

Six Key Questions When Developing a Strategy

1. **What is my goal?**
2. **What do I already know about this problem or challenge?**
3. **What steps must I take to get the job done successfully?**
4. **What possible problems might I face?**
5. **Whom can I ask for help or advice?**
6. **What research can I do to find out more information?**

Imagine that Margarita, a good friend in your class, tells you she wants to become a veterinarian. She asks you what you think she should do to achieve this goal. Use the questions to help her develop an effective strategy.

A Strategy for Margarita

Margarita's long-term goal: ______________________________

What might she already know about being a veterinarian?

1. ______________________________
2. ______________________________
3. ______________________________

What specific steps could she take to improve her chances of achieving her goal?

Her Grades:

1. ______________________________

2. ______________________________

3. ______________________________

Impressing her teachers with her effort, attitude, motivation, and ability:

1. ______________________________

2. ______________________________

3. ______________________________

4. ______________________________

Planning her education (courses):

1. ______________________________

2. ______________________________

3. ______________________________

Job training:

1. ______________________________

2. ______________________________

What problems might Margarita encounter?

1. ______________________________

2. ______________________________

3. ______________________________

Whom could she ask for help or advice?

1. ______________________________

2. ______________________________

3. ______________________________

How would you evaluate the strategy you created for Margarita?

1	2	3	4	5	6	7	8	9	10
Not Smart			**Fairly Smart**					**Very Smart**	

If Margarita followed your plan, how would you rate her chances of becoming a veterinarian?

1	2	3	4	5	6	7	8	9	10
Not Good			**Fairly Good**					**Excellent**	

Creating Your Own Strategy

Now it's your turn to make up a strategy that will permit you to achieve a specific long-term goal. For practice, choose one of the following goals and develop a strategy for achieving it. Circle the goal you have chosen.

Become a Better Basketball Player

or

Get a Better Grade in Math or English on My Next Report Card

or

Earn a Black Belt in Karate

or

Get an "A" on the Next History Test

or

Get a Leading Part in the School Play

Steps I Would Need to Take:

1. ______________________________
2. ______________________________
3. ______________________________
4. ______________________________
5. ______________________________
6. ______________________________

Now select a **long-term goal** you would *really* like to achieve and develop a strategy for reaching your objective. Although you may have several long-term goals, just choose one for now. The goal should be something that is very important to you. You could use the long-term goal you wrote down in Unit 11 (see page 158), or you could select another goal. The goal doesn't necessarily have to involve a career. It could be to make the high school debate team. If you already know that your goal is to become an attorney, this is an opportunity for you to create a plan for achieving this goal.

Use the six key questions (see page 182) and the same step-by-step procedure you used to help Margarita achieve her goal. When you list the short-term steps necessary to attaining your long-term goal, make sure you list them in order of priority. For example, getting good grades in high school should be listed **before** going to a good college because this step must happen in order to get into a good college.

If you're having difficulty deciding on an interesting goal, you could choose one from the following list:

Possible Career Goals

Pilot
FBI Agent
Clothing Designer
Race-Car Driver
Singer
Auto Mechanic
Artist
U.S. President
Fashion Model
Airline Pilot
Clothing Designer
Teacher
Dentist
Journalist

Lawyer
College Professor
Buyer for a Department Store
Actor
Corporate President
Airplane Mechanic
Scientist
Police Officer
Archeologist
Professional Athlete
Astronaut
Judge
Physician
Heavy-Equipment Operator

Nurse
Fireman
Military Officer
Engineer
Psychologist
Dancer
Veterinarian
Teacher
Writer
Architect
Musician
Entrepreneur
Movie Producer
Contractor

My Strategy

My Long-Term Goal: ____

Steps to get the job done successfully and achieve the goal: (These are your short-term goals.)

My grades:

1. ____
2. ____
3. ____

Impressing my teachers:

1. ____
2. ____

Planning my education (courses):

1. ____
2. ____
3. ____

Job training:

1. ____
2. ____

What problems might I face?

1. ____
2. ____
3. ____

Whom could I ask for help?

1. ____
2. ____

If you use this strategy, how would you rate your chances of achieving your objective?

1 2 3 4 5 6 7 8 9 10

Poor Fairly Good Very Good

How would you evaluate your strategy?

1 2 3 4 5 6 7 8 9 10

Poor Fairly Good Very Good

Changing Course

Let's say Margarita uses the strategy for becoming a veterinarian that you created for her. In her senior year of high school, she changes her mind and decides she no longer wants to become a vet. She decides instead that she wants to become a scientist.

Do you think she wasted her time following her original strategy because she decided to change her goal? **Yes No Not Sure**

Why? ____

____

____

____

Would it be difficult for her to create a new strategy to achieve her new long-term goal?

Yes No Not Sure

Do you think it's OK for kids to change their goals? **Yes No Not Sure**

Is there value in establishing long-term and short-term goals, even though they might change?

Yes No Not Sure

Why? ____

____

____

____

____

What is the value of having a strategy? ____________________

____

____

____

Mastery: More Practice Developing Strategies

Create a strategy for conserving natural resources at your school (water, paper, fuel, pencils, electricity, etc.) Remember to define your objective (long-term goal). Use the **six key questions** (page 182) to help you develop your plan.

A Strategy for Conserving Natural Resources at School

Long-Term Goal: ____________________

What I already know about conserving natural resources:

1. ____________________
2. ____________________
3. ____________________
4. ____________________
5. ____________________
6. ____________________

What steps could improve the chances of achieving this goal?

1. ____________________
2. ____________________
3. ____________________
4. ____________________
5. ____________________
6. ____________________

What problems might be encountered?

1. ____________________
2. ____________________
3. ____________________

4. ____
5. ____
6. ____

Who might be asked for help or advice?

1. ____
2. ____
3. ____
4. ____

If you follow this strategy, how would you rate the chances of your school being able to conserve natural resources?

1 2 3 4 5 6 7 8 9 10

Poor Fairly Good Very Good

A Strategy that Failed

Colin and Ryan were freshmen, and both were on the junior-varsity baseball team. The two friends wanted to make varsity in their sophomore year. The problem was that there were eight excellent players on the j.v. squad, and the boys were far from certain that they would be selected by the varsity coach. To improve their chances and improve their skills, they decided in September that they would go to a one-week baseball camp the following summer. Ex-professional players ran the camp, and it was highly regarded by both the j.v and varsity coaches.

Their parents agreed to let them go, but they insisted that the boys pay half the tuition. Each boys' share would be $250.00. They decided that they would have to begin saving their allowance money and the money they earned doing chores and washing cars. Unfortunately, every week something would come up, and they would spend their money. They would go to the movies or ice-skating rink, or they might rent a video or go to the mall and buy food and clothes. Buying presents for birthdays and Christmas also used up a great deal of their money. In March, Colin discovered that he had been able to save only $40.00, and Ryan discovered he had only saved $30.00. The deposit for the camp--$150 for each boy--was due in two weeks. Both boys realized they didn't have enough time left to save the money they needed.

Why didn't the strategy work? ______________________________

____

____

Use the **six key questions** to create a strategy that would have worked.

A Revised Strategy for Colin and Ryan

Long-Term Goal: ______________________________

What the boys probably already knew about saving money:

1. ______________________________
2. ______________________________
3. ______________________________
4. ______________________________

Steps the boys might take to get the job done successfully: (These are their short-term goals).

1. ______________________________
2. ______________________________
3. ______________________________
4. ______________________________

What problems might the boys face?

1. ______________________________
2. ______________________________
3. ______________________________
4. ______________________________

Whom could the boys ask for advice or help?

1. ______________________________
2. ______________________________
3. ______________________________
4. ______________________________

If the boys follow this strategy, how would you rate their chances of saving enough money to go to baseball camp?

1	2	3	4	5	6	7	8	9	10
Poor			**Fairly Good**					**Very Good**	

Reviewing What's Smart and What's Not Smart

Take a few minutes to complete the following checklist.

Thinking-Smart Checklist

	SMART	NOT-SO-SMART	DUMB
He continually loses his school assignments.	_____	_____	_____
She spends extra time practicing for her piano recital.	_____	_____	_____
He writes key facts on index cards to help prepare for the history test.	_____	_____	_____
He doesn't refer to his assignment sheet and forgets to study for the math quiz.	_____	_____	_____
She fails to review her previous tests when preparing for her social-studies final.	_____	_____	_____
He pays a student to write an English report for him.	_____	_____	_____
He writes a thumb-nail outline before answering an essay question on a test.	_____	_____	_____
He and a friend make up a practice test before the mid-term.	_____	_____	_____
She takes an hour to reorganize her messy binder.	_____	_____	_____
She talks on the phone for two hours and doesn't complete her Spanish assignment.	_____	_____	_____
He fails to schedule enough time to proofread his book report.	_____	_____	_____
He carefully goes through his class notes and textbook notes and highlights main ideas in one color and details in another.	_____	_____	_____
She takes notes on the unit while studying for the test.	_____	_____	_____

	SMART	NOT-SO-SMART	DUMB
He makes up a study schedule.	_____	_____	_____
He doesn't hand in his math assignment on time.	_____	_____	_____
She doesn't understand the math problems and asks the teacher for help.	_____	_____	_____
He tries to figure out a way to steal the science test from the teacher's desk drawer.	_____	_____	_____
She decides to mind-map the new government unit.	_____	_____	_____
She goes over her work one more time before handing in the algebra test.	_____	_____	_____
He practices his jump shots, foul shots, and lay-ups thirty minutes each afternoon during the off-season.	_____	_____	_____
She studies the wrong material for the test.	_____	_____	_____
She takes the time to rewrite her sloppy assignment.	_____	_____	_____
She refuses to accept a ride home from a football game because she thinks the boy is drunk.	_____	_____	_____
He takes money from his mom's purse.	_____	_____	_____
She goes to a party where kids are likely to be doing drugs.	_____	_____	_____

What I Have Learned about Strategies

List the **six key questions** you should ask *before* creating a strategy:

1. ____
2. ____
3. ____
4. ____
5. ____
6. ____

Unit 14

Cause and Effect

Considering the Possibilities

Kelsey really wanted to go to the mall with her best friend Meagan and Meagan's older sister on Saturday. She desperately needed new school clothes. The summer vacation would be over in less than two weeks, and Kelsey hadn't done any shopping yet. Meagan's older sister had her driver's license, and the plan was for the three girls to get to the mall at 10:00 AM on Saturday. They would browse in the stores, have lunch, and finish their shopping after lunch.

There was only one problem: Kelsey didn't have enough money to buy what she needed. Her parent had promised to give her some, but since she had a summer job, they also insisted that she use a portion of the money she earned to buy school clothes. Unfortunately, Kelsey had trouble saving. As soon as she received her paycheck, she would go out and spend most of it.

Kelsey had only managed to put away about $75.00. Her parents had agreed to give her $250.00. That meant she would have a total of $325.00, and that wouldn't buy very much. She wanted jeans, shirts, two pairs of shoes, two sweaters, two pairs of slacks, and at least two new outfits for school. Even if she bought things on sale, she figured that she would need a minimum of $375.00 to get what she wanted.

During the summer, Kelsey's dad had told her to save some of her earnings because she might need it later. Kelsey hadn't followed his advice, and now she wished she had. She desperately needed clothes, but she didn't want to ask her parents for more money. She knew what they would say: “We told you to save your money.” She hated it when her parents lectured her.

Then Kelsey had an idea. Her mother kept “emergency money” in a box hidden on the top shelf of the cabinet in the bathroom. “Maybe I could borrow $50 and put the money back after I get my final paycheck next week,” she thought.

“Mom would never even realize that the money is gone. It's really not stealing since I'm going to return it,” she decided.

Believing that the problem was solved, Kelsey felt much better. She would borrow the money on Friday while her mom was grocery shopping.

Later that day, Kelsey became less enthusiastic about her plan. Something felt wrong, and she felt uneasy. That night she had trouble sleeping. In the morning, she decided that she couldn’t take the money. Even though she planned on returning the money, it still felt like stealing.

Kelsey decided to admit to her parents that she didn’t have enough money to get the clothes she needed. Although she expected that they would be upset, she would ask to borrow an extra $50.00. If they agreed to lend her the money, she would promise to pay it back in eight days after she got paid. If they didn't agree to lend her the money, she would be disappointed, but she would just have to handle it. She knew it would be unpleasant to deal with her parents’ “We told you so,” but this was better than taking money that didn’t belong to her.

Kelsey had learned a lesson. Her dad was right about saving money.

Examining Decisions

In the story, when Kelsey realized that she didn’t have enough money to buy the clothes she needed, she made a decision about how to handle the problem. The decision had to do with her mom. Underline this decision. Then in your own words, describe the decision below.

Kelsey’s Decision #1: ____

How would you evaluate the wisdom this decision?

1 2 3 4 5 6 7 8 9 10

Not Smart Fairly Smart Very Smart

Why did you rate her decision in this way? ________________________________

____

____

If Kelsey had followed through with her original decision, and if she had taken the money, write down three possible consequences.

Consequence # 1 ____

____

Consequence # 2 ____

____

Consequence # 3 ____

____

After much thought and a restless night, Kelsey had second thoughts and made another decision. Go back to the story, underline this decision, and then describe the decision in your own words.

Kelsey's Decision #2: ____

How would you evaluate the wisdom this second decision?

1 2 3 4 5 6 7 8 9 10

Not Smart **Fairly Smart** **Very Smart**

Why did you rate her decision in this way? ____

____

____

Kelsey then changed her mind and made another decision. Go back to the story, underline the third decision and describe it in your own words.

Kelsey's Decision #3: ____

How would you evaluate the wisdom of this third decision?

1 2 3 4 5 6 7 8 9 10

Not Smart **Fairly Smart** **Very Smart**

Why did you rate her decision in this way? ____

____

____

The story doesn't indicate the consequence of this third decision. Write down as many potential consequences (positive and/or negative) of this new decision as you can. Then indicate whether you believe each consequence is possible or probable

Potential Consequence ______________________________

Possible **Probable**

Potential Consequence ______________________________

Possible **Probable**

Potential Consequence ______________________________

Possible **Probable**

Potential Consequence ______________________________

Possible **Probable**

Potential Consequence ______________________________

Possible **Probable**

Why do you think Kelsey made decision #3? ______________________________

____

____

Do you think Kelsey learned anything from struggling with her dilemma? If so, what did she learn? ______________________________

____

____

____

Considering the Consequences

Most decisions produce consequences. For example, the likely consequence of you and a friend deciding to toss a football back and forth near the living room window is that the window will be broken. If this happens, there will probably be an additional consequence. You'll get into trouble, and your parents will say: "You didn't use your head!"

One person may think about the possible consequences before he begins to toss a football near a window. He may decide not to play football, or he may decide to play somewhere else. Someone else may not bother to consider the risk. Both of these kids are making decisions. They are *choosing* either to consider the consequences or to disregard the consequences.

Decisions can come back to haunt you. For example, you may decide not to hand in an assignment and, as a consequence, get an F on the assignment. "No big deal," you might think.

"It's only one homework assignment." At the end of the semester, however, your teacher may have her own decision to make. Based on your test scores, she could give you either a B- or a C+ in the course. Concluding that you have been working hard, she decides to give you a B-. Then she looks at her grade book, sees the F you received for not handing in your assignment, and changes her mind. She give you a C+, and you end up paying a much bigger price for your decision than you thought your would.

By training yourself to be aware of potential consequences, you can reduce the risk of disaster. Knowing that your skateboard has a loose wheel and deciding to do something about fixing the problem is certainly preferable to minimizing the potential danger or being lazy and choosing not to repair the wheel. In either case, you are responsible for your decisions and you are responsible for the consequences of your decisions.

In the exercise below, draw a line from the decision to the consequence that you would expect to result from the decision.

DECISION	POSSIBLE CONSEQUENCE
1. Creating a study schedule	a. drowning
2. Forgetting to write down your assignments	b. pleasing your parents
3. Taking notes on a science unit	c. making the varsity
4. Not studying for a mid-term	d. losing your parents' trust
5. Spreading nasty rumors about kids in class	e. improving your game
6. Experimenting with drugs	f. having it stolen
7. Working hard in soccer practice	g. working more efficiently
8. Applying early for a summer job	h. upsetting your mom
9. Not using your seatbelt	i. becoming addicted
10. Lying to your parents	j. getting a low grade
11. Checking your report for spelling errors	k. flunking
12. Leaving your skateboard in the park	l. getting a better grade on the report
13. Stealing from a department store	m. being unpopular
14. Doing your chores without being reminded	n. not knowing what homework to do
15. Practicing your volleyball serve	o. understanding and recalling information
16. Plagiarizing on a term paper	p. getting arrested
17. Trying to cross a fast-moving, stream	q. increasing the likelihood of being hired
18. Leaving dirty dishes in your bedroom	r. increasing the chances of a serious injury

The Decision Point

Have you ever heard the expression *"That's par for the course"?* The expression was borrowed from golf, but the words have come to mean that what has happened is to be expected. Well, having to make difficult decisions is par for the course of being a human being. You cannot go through life without occasionally confronting some tough choices.

As you struggle to make the right decision, you will ideally evaluate the arguments in favor of a particular choice (these are sometimes referred to as the "pluses" or the "pros") and the arguments against the choice (these are called the "minuses" or the "cons"). The procedure is usually referred to as *"weighing the pros and cons"* or *"weighing the pluses or minuses."* You would also think about the possible consequences for each option. In some cases, this weighing process can happen very quickly, and in other cases you may need to wrestle for days or even weeks with the issues involved in an important decision. Deciding what college to attend is a perfect example of a major decision that would require a great deal of time and careful analytical thinking.

Finally, you arrive at a **decision point**, and you make your choice. For example, you may see a sweater you really like in a department store. You try it on in the dressing room, and you love the way it fits and looks. You notice that the security tag has been removed, and for an instant, you might be tempted to put it under your coat and steal it. But then your values and your parents' training kick in, and you realize it's wrong to steal. You also think about what could happen if you are caught shoplifting. You would get into serious trouble. The store manager would call the police, and you would be taken to the police station. Your parents would be called, and they would have to come to the police station. They would be incredibly upset and disappointed in you. They would also have to hire a lawyer, and you would face the possibility of being locked up in juvenile hall and having a criminal record.

In the preceding hypothetical situation (that is, a situation that might occur), you arrived at the decision point when you decide either to steal or not steal the sweater. If you make the wrong choice at this critically important decision point, your life might be forever changed. If you have a police record, you might not be accepted the college of your choice. You might not be able to enlist in the army or become a police officer. You might not be able to become a lawyer. These are clearly serious possible consequences, and they are the result of a flawed decision at the critically important decision point.

Deciding whether you want a chocolate or vanilla sundae also involves making a choice, but this choice is obviously very different from deciding if you want to try a drug offered to you by someone at a party. The first decision is not especially important. The second decision is monumentally important.

Kids who are in the habit of thinking about what they are doing will carefully weigh the pros and cons when they arrive at an important decision point. Because they are in the habit of weighing the pros and cons and considering the potential consequences of their actions, they would undoubtedly decide not to steal a sweater from a department store for three key reasons:

- Shoplifting is morally wrong,
- The risks are too great, especially given the ever-present security cameras.
- The consequences for getting caught are too severe.

Sometimes you may need to wrestle with a particular choice for hours, days, or even weeks and months. An example might be deciding whether or not to break-up with a boyfriend or girlfriend. Sometimes you add the pros and cons, think about the consequences, and know what the right decision almost immediately. An example would be deciding not to steal. You may see a really neat parked car that has the key in the ignition. For an instant you may be tempted to take it for a joyride. You think about what it would be like to be arrested and "booked." You think about your parents' disillusionment and shame. You think about your own shame. Once you go through this analytical thinking process, not taking the car becomes a "no brainer."

Identifying the Decision Point

As you read the story below, underline each **decision point**. Number the decision points that are described in the order in which they occurred.

Evan's Study Procedure

Evan didn't study for his weekly science quiz. He ran out of time. When he got home from school, he played baseball with his friends until dinner. Then after dinner, he watched his favorite sitcoms. When his mom asked if he had done his homework, he told her that he had completed it in school. This was not true. When the sitcoms he liked were over at 8:00 PM, he switched channels and began watching a movie until 9:30. His mother reminded him that it was time for bed, and he reluctantly turned off the TV, went to his room, and got ready for bed. He planned to study the next morning on the school bus, but then he started talking with his friends and before he knew it the bus had arrived at school. Evan hoped that he would somehow pass the test, but he knew from past experience that when he didn't study, he would usually get an F.

Reread the story and underline and number each of Evan's decisions. You should find at least five. Now predict the potential consequence of each decision, and circle *possible* or *probable.*

Consequence of Decision #1: ______________________________

Possible **Probable**

Consequence of Decision #2: ______________________________

Possible **Probable**

Consequence of Decision #3: ______________________________

Possible **Probable**

Consequence of Decision #4: ______________________________

Possible **Probable**

Consequence of Decision #5: ______________________________

Possible **Probable**

Describing a Decision Point in Your Own Life

Describe a time in your life when you arrived at a **decision point** and made a choice or several choices that involved possible or probable consequences. Write the experience below. **Don't write down the consequences of your choices yet!** *If you can't think of an experience, you can make up a story.* You might want to begin the story: "When I was ___ years old, I ...." or "Last year, when my sister and I were ....." You might, for example, write: "When I was seven, I was in the supermarket with my father, and I wanted some candy. My dad was looking for something on a shelf, and he was not paying attention to what I was doing. I glanced around to see if anyone was looking, and I reached for the candy. I was about to put the candy in my pocket. At the last minute, I decided that stealing was wrong and that I might get caught. I put the candy back on the shelf."

A Decision Point in My Life

Underline the **decision point** (or **decision points** if there are more than one) in your story, and write down the consequence of the decision (or decisions) that you made.

Consequence of Decision #1: ______

Consequence of Decision #2: ______

Consequence of Decision #3: ______

Of course, if the story you wrote about was real, the consequences of your decision or decisions have already happened. If the situation occurred in the past, you most likely know the outcome. We can describe this outcome as the **actual consequence**. While the situation was evolving, however, you might have been able to predict the *possible* or *probable* consequences of your decision or decisions. For example, if you described in your story that you cheated on a test and got caught, you could have predicted that getting caught was a distinctly possible consequence. Had you weighed the pros and cons and had you considered the potential consequence *before* you made your final decision, you could have avoided the outcome. This is called **"thinking about the consequences."**

Future Thinking

Teenagers who think about the consequences of their decisions and actions **before** they act operate very differently from kids who act mindlessly. When you are in the habit of considering the possible or probable consequences in advance, you will discover that you can avoid many head-on collisions in life. You are far less likely to:

- get poor grades
- make poor choices
- make your parents or teachers angry
- alienate your friends
- get into trouble
- be punished
- have accidents
- run out of time
- run out of money
- be lazy
- break the law

Defining Cause and Effect

You may have heard people use the expression "cause and effect." This is another way of describing "thinking about the consequences." The **cause** is the decision. The **effect** is the consequence or result of the decision.

> ***Remember:***
>
> ***You are thinking smart when you get into the habit of thinking about cause and effect before you act!***

Practice Figuring Out the Effect (or Consequence)

Each situation described below describes a decision (the **cause**). Decide what the **consequence** (or **effect**) of each decision might be and write it down. Then circle if this effect is **possible** (may happen) or **probable** (likely to happen).

You forget to write down your science assignment.

Effect: ____

Possible or Probable

You take the time to proofread your book report carefully.

Effect: ____

Possible or Probable

A friend plagiarizes an article in a magazine.

Effect: ____

Possible or Probable

You work out hard during the off-season to keep in shape.

Effect: ____

Possible or Probable

A friend takes a hunting knife to school.

Effect: ____

Possible or Probable

You develop a careful strategy for studying for your history mid-term, and you spend one hour every evening taking notes, reviewing, and memorizing important information.

Effect: ____

Possible or Probable

You volunteer to help your dad paint the house.

Effect: ____

Possible or Probable

You forget to bring home your textbooks on the night before a big test.

Effect: ____

Possible or Probable

You don't check how deep the water is before you dive off a tree limb into a river.

Effect: ____

Possible or Probable

You help your friend cheat on a test.

Effect: ____

Possible or Probable

You begin working on your term paper three weeks before it is due.

Effect: ____

Possible or Probable

The decisions described above are called the C________________________.

The consequences can also be called the E__________________

Practice Figuring Out the Cause

Figure out the **cause** (or the decision) that produced the following consequences

The car engine starts to overheat while you are driving on the highway.

Cause: ____

You get a bad grade on your science midterm.

Cause: ____

You get an A- on your math homework.

Cause: ____

The teacher gets angry at you in class.

Cause: ____

You don't know what your science homework assignment is.

Cause: ______________________________

Your coat is stolen from your locker.

Cause: ______________________________

The soccer coach lets you play the entire game.

Cause: ______________________________

You don't submit your term paper on time.

Cause: ______________________________

Your parents don't trust you.

Cause: ______________________________

A friend has his laptop stolen in school.

Cause: ______________________________

You get a good letter of recommendation from your science teacher that you include with your college application.

Cause: ______________________________

What Would You Do?

Describe how you would react to the following situations, predict the effect or consequence, and indicate whether the effect is *possible* or *probable.*

You're competing in a skateboard tournament. Your parents have told you that you must wear your helmet, but you don't want to because you think it makes you look like a wimp.

Your Decision: ______________________________

____

Effect: ______________________________

Possible or Probable

You see your little brother and his friends throwing rocks at each other in the park.

Your Decision: ______________________________

____

Effect: ______________________________

Possible or Probable

You're playing basketball, and the referee calls you for a foul. You are convinced he is wrong.

Your Decision: ______________________________

____

Effect: ______________________________

Possible or Probable

You are on a camping trip. You are about to go on a hike, but you don't want to take your camera and wallet with you in case you fall in the stream.

Your Decision: ______________________________

____

Effect: ______________________________

Possible or Probable

Mastery: More Practice Figuring Out the Cause

Read each statement and choose the likely **cause** from the list at the end of the exercise.

1. ____, and she received a good grade.
2. ____, and he was bitten.
3. ____________________________________, and he didn't know what his homework was.
4. __________________________________, and she didn't get soaked at the football game.
5. ____, and he got fired.
6. ____, and it was stolen.
7. ______________________________________, and she lost ten pounds.
8. ___________________________________, and she missed the school bus.
9. _______________________________, and he was expelled.
10. ______________________________, and he corrected six careless errors.
11. ___________________________________, and he forgot his socks.
12. ___________________________________, and the teacher flunked her.
13. ______________________________, and his parents were very proud.
14. ____, and they got lost.
15. ____________________________________ and had to go to detention after school
16. _________________________ and had enough money for the trip.
17. _______________________________________ and the man was arrested by the police.

a. She took her umbrella
b. He teased the dog
c. He checked over his math assignment
d. He left his wallet on the beach blanket
e. They were talking in class
f. She took notes and studied hard
g. She overslept
h. She cheated on the test
i. She saved her babysitting money.
j. He didn't record his assignments
k. He took a weapon to school
l. He made the honor roll at school
m. She stopped eating candy and drinking soda
n. He was disrespectful to his boss
o. He didn't allow enough time to pack
p. They didn't have a map
q. He told his teacher about the man selling drugs

Identifying the Cause and the Effect

Make up a cause and then fill in the effect. You can write down a fun **cause**, but make sure the **effect** makes sense. For example:

He __________ the ball, and it ____________________________.

He *threw* the ball, and it *broke the window*. (serious)

He *hid* the ball, and it *drove his friend crazy!* (fun)

The supervisor at work ____, and she gave Courtney ____.

She ___________________________________, and her mom ___________________________.

He ______________________ the test, and his teacher ______________________________.

The varsity ______________________________, so the coach ______________.

Because ________________________, they lost ___________________________________.

When the teacher ______________________________, the kids began ________________.

The team won the championship ____ because the players ____.

The coach ___________________________, because he had ___________________________ __________________________________ during practice.

The student changed ____, and she ___________ ____.

The kids at the party began _________________________________, and the neighbors _____________________.

He __________________________________, and his sister ___________________________.

The coach increased _________________________, and the team _____________________.

Applying Cause and Effect to Your Own Life

What Would You Do?

Your friend comes to your house on a motorcycle he borrowed from his uncle. He tells you his uncle doesn't actually know he has borrowed the motorcycle, but if he did, your friend is certain it would be OK. He asks if you want to go for a ride with him.

Your Decision: ____

Probable Effect: ____

____

Evaluate your decision:

1	2	3	4	5	6	7	8	9	10

Not Smart **Fairly Smart** **Very Smart**

The teacher is writing the homework assignments on the board.

Your Decision: ____

Probable Effect: ____

____

Evaluate your decision:

1	2	3	4	5	6	7	8	9	10

Not Smart **Fairly Smart** **Very Smart**

The teacher gives the class 20 minutes of free time. Students can start doing their homework, or they can use the time to talking to each other. A great deal of homework has been assigned.

Your Decision: ____

Probable Effect: ____

____

Evaluate your decision:

1	2	3	4	5	6	7	8	9	10

Not Smart **Fairly Smart** **Very Smart**

What I Have Learned about Cause and Effect

Draw a line from the word to the correct meaning

Cause	**Consequence**
Effect	**Decision**

Define the **decision point**. ____

____

Evaluate the following decisions.

I promise my mother that I won't go to a dangerous park, but I go anyway.

1	2	3	4	5	6	7	8	9	10

Not Smart **Fairly Smart** **Very Smart**

I spend an extra hour studying for a government test.

1 2 3 4 5 6 7 8 9 10

Not Smart Fairly Smart Very Smart

I tell my parents that a party will be chaperoned when I know my friend's parents are out of town.

1 2 3 4 5 6 7 8 9 10

Not Smart Fairly Smart Very Smart

I borrow my brother's DVD player without asking permission.

1 2 3 4 5 6 7 8 9 10

Not Smart Fairly Smart Very Smart

I go to a party where I know kids will be drinking.

1 2 3 4 5 6 7 8 9 10

Not Smart Fairly Smart Very Smart

I let a friend copy a book report I wrote last year.

1 2 3 4 5 6 7 8 9 10

Not Smart Fairly Smart Very Smart

I accept a ride home from basketball practice from an acquaintance who seems drunk.

1 2 3 4 5 6 7 8 9 10

Not Smart Fairly Smart Very Smart

I agree to hold a package for a friend. He won't tell me what's inside, but he tells me that I can't tell anyone about it.

1 2 3 4 5 6 7 8 9 10

Not Smart Fairly Smart Very Smart

Unit 15

Heading Off Problems

Trouble Can Ambush You

Jennifer couldn't believe what her friend Ashley was telling her. Ashley said that she had found an open bottle of liquor in a cabinet at home, and she had decided to try some. She had ended up drinking almost two glasses and woke up the next morning with a terrible headache. Somehow she had made it to school, but she had to take three aspirin with her orange juice. She told Jennifer that she hadn't been able to concentrate all morning because of her hangover.

At first, Ashley hadn't liked the taste of the liquor but when she had mixed it with cola, it tasted OK. She said the drinks made her a bit dizzy and then her head began to swim, but she said she liked the feeling. That evening she was planning to drink the rest of the bottle. She knew where her parents kept several boxes of unopened liquor bottles, and she was planning to replace the bottle she had used. She told Jennifer her parents would never even realize that the bottle was missing. She then asked Jennifer if she wanted to try some that evening. Jennifer refused. She told her friend that she had decided not to drink until she was a lot older.

Jennifer was upset. She felt her friend was making a terrible mistake. Ashley had always been a good student who wanted to go to law school and become a judge. Jennifer was certain that if her friend started to drink, her grades would fall, and if they did, she might not even get into college, much less into law school.

Jennifer knew other kids at school who drank. She would see them at parties stumbling around, acting dumb, saying stupid things, and thinking they were really cool. It usually started with one drink when they were twelve or thirteen, and before long they were drunk every weekend. Once they got into the habit, it was very hard for them to stop. They would steal the liquor from their parents or use their allowance and get someone to buy it for them. Even though they were still kids, Jennifer suspected that many of them were already alcoholics.

Jennifer didn't know what to do. She realized Ashley was drinking because she felt it made her look and feel grown up and because she desperately wanted to be accepted by the cool crowd at school. Ashley also liked the thrill of doing something behind her parents' backs.

Jennifer decided that she had to do something to keep her friend from making a terrible mistake. She couldn't just stand by and let Ashley ruin her life! The problem was figuring out what to do. Although she didn't want to get Ashley in trouble, she was prepared to do whatever was necessary, even if it meant damaging their friendship. She had to intervene.

Examining the Story

At the end of the story, Jennifer arrived at a *decision point* about her friend's drinking and what she felt she had to do. *This was actually Jennifer's third decision.* Let's start with her first decision. Jennifer's *first decision point* occurred when Ashley asked if she wanted to drink liquor with her that evening. Go back to the story, underline the decision, and write "1" in front of it.

What was Jennifer's first decision? ____

____

1 2 3 4 5 6 7 8 9 10

Not Smart Fairly Smart Very Smart

Why did you evaluate her decision in this way? ______________________________

____

____

Jennifer actually made her second decision before she became aware that her friend had started drinking liquor. Go back to the story, underline the decision, and write "2" in front of it.

What was Jennifer's second decision? ______________________________________

____

How would you evaluate this decision?

1 2 3 4 5 6 7 8 9 10

Not Smart Fairly Smart Very Smart

Why did you evaluate her decision in this way? ____

____

____

Jennifer's *third decision point* happened at the end of the story. Go back to the story, underline the decision, and write the number "3" in front of it.

What was Jennifer's third decision? ____

____

How would you evaluate this decision?

1 2 3 4 5 6 7 8 9 10

Not Smart **Fairly Smart** **Very Smart**

Why did you evaluate the decision in this way? ____

____

____

What do you think Jennifer could do to help her friend? List as many interventions (or **causes**) as you can, describe the potential consequence (or **effect**) of each intervention, and indicate whether the consequence is *possible* or *probable*.

Possible Intervention 1: ____

Consequence: ____

Possible **Probable**

Evaluate the intervention:

1 2 3 4 5 6 7 8 9 10

Not Smart **Fairly Smart** **Very Smart**

List the pluses (or pros) and minuses (or cons) of this idea.

Pluses	**Minuses**
____________________	____________________
____________________	____________________
____________________	____________________
____________________	____________________

Possible Intervention 2: ____________________

Consequence: ____________________

Possible Probable

Evaluate the intervention:

1	2	3	4	5	6	7	8	9	10
Not Smart			Fairly Smart					Very Smart	

List the pluses (or pros) and minuses (or cons) of this idea.

Pluses	Minuses
____________________	____________________
____________________	____________________
____________________	____________________
____________________	____________________

Possible Intervention 3: ____________________

Consequence: ____________________

Possible or Probable

Evaluate the intervention:

1	2	3	4	5	6	7	8	9	10
Not Smart			Fairly Smart					Very Smart	

List the pluses (or pros) and minuses (or cons) of this idea.

Pluses	Minuses
____________________	____________________
____________________	____________________
____________________	____________________
____________________	____________________

Possible Intervention 4: ____________________

Consequence: ____________________

Possible or Probable

Evaluate the intervention:

1 2 3 4 5 6 7 8 9 10

Not Smart **Fairly Smart** **Very Smart**

List the pluses (or pros) and minuses (or cons) of this idea.

Pluses	**Minuses**
______________________	______________________
______________________	______________________
______________________	______________________
______________________	______________________

Did you write down any of these possible interventions?

1. *Jennifer could tell Ashley's parents.*
2. *Jennifer could get a group of Ashley's friends to talk to her.*
3. *Jennifer could try to convince Ashley to stop.*
4. *Jennifer could tell her own parents about Ashley's drinking.*
5. *Jennifer could talk to Ashley's older sister about the problem (assuming she has an older sister).*

(It's perfectly acceptable if you came up with different ideas, as long as the ideas make sense.)

Of the five interventions listed above, which do you think would be the most effective? #______

Why? ____

____

Do you think it would be difficult for Jennifer to intervene?

Yes **No**

Why? ____

____

Would you have had the same reaction as Jennifer if a friend of yours were making a similar error in judgment and started drinking or taking drugs? **Yes** **No** **Not Sure**

How would you have handled the situation? ______________________________

____

____

Making Tough Decisions

Have you ever faced a dilemma such as the one described above? You wanted to do the right thing, but you were afraid you might make the wrong decision? If you felt very unsure about what to do, you may have been tempted to not make any decision at all!

As you struggled with your choices, you probably considered many issues. Perhaps you were afraid that you would feel guilty. Perhaps you were afraid that you would make someone mad at you. For example, you may have seen a group of older kids that you know picking on some younger children, and you were tempted to intervene. One voice inside of you told you that saying something and helping the little kids was the right thing to do. Another voice told you not to get involved. This type of situation, which involves and tests your personal values, is referred to as a *moral dilemma* or an *ethical dilemma.*

Jennifer faced a moral dilemma as she struggled to figure out how to stop her friend from drinking. If Ashley refused to listen to her, Jennifer would have had to make some more hard choices. First, she would have to decide if she was going to intervene. If she decided that she must intervene, she would then have to decide how best to do so. As she wrestled with these difficult choices, she would undoubtedly consider whether her actions would ruin her friendship with Ashley.

Jennifer obviously didn't want to get Ashley in trouble. She didn't want to be a tattletale. She just wanted to prevent someone she liked from acting dumb.

Complete the following inventory and indicate how you would analyze the moral dilemma that Jennifer faced.

Moral/Ethical-Dilemma Inventory

	Yes	No	Maybe
Do you think Jennifer should intervene even though whatever she did would probably make Ashley mad?	____	____	____
Would Ashley feel betrayed if Jennifer told Ashley's parents or her own parents?	____	____	____
Would Ashley be justified in feeling betrayed?	____	____	____
If Jennifer does tell Ashley's parents, do you think she is doing this to be mean?	____	____	____
Do you think that Jennifer would get over being mad at her?	____	____	____
Do teenagers sometimes have to make hard choices that are painful or unpopular?	____	____	____
Do teenagers ever have to take an action that might make a friend mad because they really care about the friend?	____	____	____
Would you feel guilty if you do something your friend doesn't like even though you believe this is in your friend's best interest?	____	____	____
Would you be willing to make a hard choice you felt was right, if your action made a friend mad?	____	____	____

Doing the Right Thing

Let's assume you find a wallet in the street. There's money inside, and you're tempted to keep it. Describe how you would decide what's the right thing to do when you are faced with this type of moral or ethical dilemma. ____

____

____

____

____

____

____

____

At some point in your life you have probably struggled with a moral or ethical dilemma similar to the situation described above. Perhaps you saw someone cheat on a test, or you saw someone steal from a locker at school. Perhaps you saw someone get into trouble for something you or a friend did. You struggled to make the right choice about what to do. Think back about a moral dilemma you faced in your own life. Don't tell what you did yet. Just describe the situation. If you can't think of an actual moral dilemma that you faced, you can make up one.____

____

____

____

What choice did you finally make? (Although you might make a different choice today, describe what you *actually did* at the time.)

____

____

____

____

Evaluate how ethical your choice was:

1 2 3 4 5 6 7 8 9 10

Not Ethical Fairly Ethical Very Ethical

If you think you would make a different choice today, describe what you would do.

____

____

____

____

____

Using Your Head to Avoid Problems

Moral and ethical dilemmas can create turmoil and stress in your life as you struggle to do what is right. Of course, not every difficult choice involves a moral dilemma. Many problems can be solved and many important decisions can be made wisely if you:

- carefully analyze the situation
- apply logic
- are aware of potential consequences
- think strategically

When faced with tough choices that could produce potentially painful consequences, the failure to think clearly and analytically could be disastrous. Acting without thinking significantly increases the likelihood that you will make the wrong decision and have repeated painful collisions in life.

Evaluate the following situations and describe how you would react.

Your best friend is cutting class and not studying.

Why would you be concerned? ______________________________

____

What could you do?

1. ______________________________
2. ______________________________
3. ______________________________

You are walking through the park with your friends, and some younger kids begin throwing rocks at each other.

Why would you be concerned? ______________________________

____

What could you do?

1. ______________________________
2. ______________________________
3. ______________________________

You see your friend steal money from her mother's purse.

Why would you be concerned? ______________________________

____

What could you do?

1. ______________________________

2. ______________________________

3. ______________________________

A friend asks you tell a lie to his parents so that he can go to a party that they have forbidden him to attend.

Why would you be concerned? ______________________________

____

What could you do?

1. ______________________________

2. ______________________________

3. ______________________________

Re-Examining the Thinking-Smart Checklist

In Unit 13 you completed a **THINKING-SMART CHECKLIST**. At the time, you weren't asked to give your reasons for marking "Smart," "Not-So-Smart," or "Dumb" after each statement. Turn back to the checklist (pages 191-192) and look at your responses again.

If you want to change some of your original answers, go ahead. Perhaps you now see things differently. If some of your attitudes have changed, this indicates that you have learned new things about yourself and about thinking smart.

If you would like to make changes, choose four of your original responses. Copy the statements from the checklist below. Use a pen (or colored pencil) to indicate your original response and a pencil (or a different colored pen) to indicate your new response. Then write down the reason for making the change.

Altering Responses on Thinking-Smart Checklist

	Smart	Not-So-Smart	Dumb
1. ______________________	_____	_____	_____

Reason for changing response ______________________________

____

2. ____ _____ ______ _____

Reason for changing response ____

____

3. ____ _____ ______ _____

Reason for changing response ____

____

4. ____ _____ ______ _____

Reason for changing response ____

____

Mastery: More Practice Avoiding Problems

You've practiced thinking about the consequences of your decisions and applying cause-and-effect principles. You realize that you not only need to apply these principles to your schoolwork, but also to situations outside of school. You also realize that by getting into the habit of thinking about what might happen when you make a decision, you reduce the risk of making a serious miscalculation that could cause you a great deal of grief in your life. For example, if someone offered you drugs at a party, you would be smart enough to recognize the potentially catastrophic consequences of agreeing to try them. You would realize that you could easily become addicted and ruin your life!

The same principles apply if a friend were to suggest you break into someone's house. You're too smart to do something that dumb. Although this person may pressure you to go along with the scheme, you know that the consequences of getting caught would be terrible! You would not only have a guilty conscience, but if you did get caught, you realize that you could end up in jail. You would think about what it would be like to be fingerprinted and put in a cell. You would think about how upset your parents would be. They would then have to spend a great deal of money to hire a good attorney, and you would have to appear before a judge in court. You would think about what it would be like to spend several months locked up in juvenile hall. You would think about how embarrassed you would be when you returned to school. You would also think about the fact that your chances of being accepted at a good college and pursuing a career would probably be ruined. Because you have learned to consider the possible and probable consequences of your actions before you act, you would avoid trouble and resist the pressure to do something illegal. In so doing, you are not only thinking smarter, you are acting morally.

Thinking smart and strategically is something you have to work at all the time. When you fail to think about cause and effect and you fail to consider the potential consequences, you significantly increase the chances of making bad decisions. Kids who never develop the habit of using their heads continually find themselves in trouble. These kids need to learn how to press their "thinking-smart button" before they make important decisions or act impulsively.

To make certain you understand the principles of thinking smart, read the following story and answer the questions at the end of the story.

The Plan That Backfired

Kyle was certain that his plan would work. Rather than study for the science mid-term that would be given on Monday, he proposed to his best friend Keith that they steal the test from the teacher's desk on Friday after school. They would take the test to the copy store, photocopy it, and return it to Mr. Parker's desk before he even realized it was missing.

Keith wasn't sure Kyle's plan was such a great idea. It seemed too risky, but he didn't want to spend five or six hours studying for the test. He wanted to play basketball, go skate boarding with his friends, go to a party on Saturday night, and watch football on Sunday afternoon. Kyle assured his friend that Mr. Parker never locked his desk drawer. He also left the room open for the janitor. Mr. Parker's room was the last one cleaned after school. Kyle told Keith that the janitor never got to the room before 5:00 PM. That gave them almost an hour and a half to copy the test and return it to Mr. Parker's desk drawer.

The boys made their decision. They would steal the test. Both boys were thrilled with how clever they were, and they were excited about not having to study over the weekend.

Everything went according to plan. From their hiding place behind some lockers, they saw Mr. Parker leave his room at 3:30 and head to the staff parking lot. They waited five minutes, and then they slipped unnoticed into the classroom. They opened the drawer and were searching through it for the test when the doorknob turned and the door opened.

What do you think happened? ____

Probable Possible

Why do you think it happened? ____________________

How would you evaluate the boys' decision to steal the test?

1 2 3 4 5 6 7 8 9 10

Not Smart Fairly Smart Very Smart

If Keith had serious misgivings about Kyle's plan, what could he have done?

1. ____________________
2. ____________________
3. ____________________

How would you evaluate the strategy you've suggested?

1 2 3 4 5 6 7 8 9 10

Not Smart Fairly Smart Very Smart

What Would You Do?

Your friend suggests you break into the elementary school and paint graffiti on the walls.

How would you rate this idea?

1 2 3 4 5 6 7 8 9 10

Not Smart Fairly Smart Very Smart

Why would you be concerned? ____________________

____

____

What are the potential consequences?

1. ____________________
2. ____________________
3. ____________________

On a hike you discover a stream. It's hot and you and your friend decide to go for a swim. Your friend challenges you to dive head first from a tree limb that is hanging over a stream.

How would you rate this idea?

1 2 3 4 5 6 7 8 9 10

Not Smart Fairly Smart Very Smart

Why would you be concerned? ____________________

____

____

What are the potential consequences?

1. ____________________
2. ____________________
3. ____________________

A friend who is a very strong swimmer asks you to swim far out into the ocean with her. You are an average swimmer. You've heard that there are riptides and an undertow at this particular beach.

How would you rate this idea?

1 2 3 4 5 6 7 8 9 10

Not Smart **Fairly Smart** **Very Smart**

Why would you be concerned? ____________________

____

____

What are the potential consequences?

1. ____________________
2. ____________________
3. ____________________

Your older brother's friend offers to give you a ride to the mall in his car, but you think he's high on drugs

How would you rate this idea?

1 2 3 4 5 6 7 8 9 10

Not Smart **Fairly Smart** **Very Smart**

Why would you be concerned? ____________________

____

____

What are the potential consequences?

1. ____________________
2. ____________________
3. ____________________

A friend suggests that you help her cheat on a test.

How would you rate this idea?

1	2	3	4	5	6	7	8	9	10
Not Smart				**Fairly Smart**				**Very Smart**	

Why would you be concerned? ______________________________

____

____

What are the potential consequences?

1. ______________________________
2. ______________________________
3. ______________________________

What I Have Learned about Avoiding Problems

	True	False
A decision point is like a fork in the road, and you have to choose a path.	____	____
Each cause or action has a potential effect or consequence.	____	____
By thinking about what might happen before you make an important decision, you can usually avoid serious mistakes.	____	____
At important decision points, you need to weigh the pros (pluses) and cons (minuses) carefully.	____	____
When making difficult decisions, just be guided by what feels right.	____	____
Too much analytical thinking can cloud your judgment.	____	____
If you simply hope for the best, things will usually turn out OK.	____	____
You can't really have any fun in life if you are always thinking about potential consequences.	____	____
When you are faced with a moral or ethical dilemma, you should just act spontaneously.	____	____
You should never make a decision that is not popular with your friends.	____	____
Repeated miscalculations can create major problems.	____	____
People who don't think for themselves and who are easily influenced by others often find themselves in serious trouble.	____	____
Live exclusively in the present and let the future take care of itself.	____	____

Unit 16

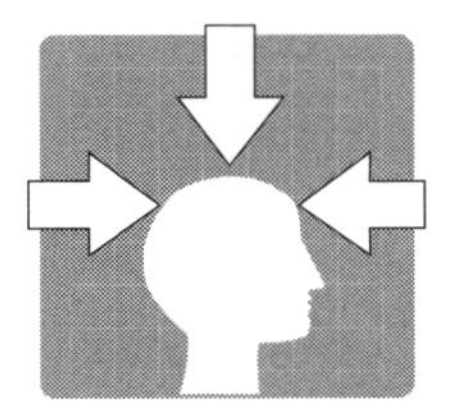

Power-Thinking

Generating Maximum Brain Power

Caitlin couldn't wait for school to be over. There were only ten more days until summer vacation started!

The soon-to-be sophomore was going to have a busy summer. Caitlin planned on enrolling in a junior-lifeguard training program at the YMCA, and she was going to take a computer class and a modern dance class at the community center. She was also planning to do a lot of babysitting so that she could save money for the volleyball camp she wanted to attend during the second week of August.

It had had been a good year for Caitlin. Her grades had improved, and all of her teachers had repeatedly complimented her for her good work. Her parents were delighted with the grades she received on her last report card, and Caitlin was certain she would do even better on her final report card. Because of her improvement, her resource specialist had informed her that this would be her last semester.

Caitlin took out the paper on which she had written her goals at the beginning of the school year. She was curious to see which objectives she had achieved and which had changed during the last nine months. As she reviewed the form, she felt like patting herself on the back.

My Long-Term Goals

1. Make the varsity volleyball team
2. Go to a good college on a volleyball scholarship
3. Make the Olympic volleyball squad and win a medal
4. Become a marine biologist
5. Get married and have two kids
6. Have a home on a hill overlooking the Pacific Ocean

My Short-Term Goals

1. Get an A- in science and B's in my other subjects on my next report card
2. Convince my volleyball coach that I am working hard, making progress, and deserve to be on the varsity
3. Improve my serves, spikes, and passing
4. Play at least a half-hour during each j.v. volleyball game
5. Get a new computer.

None of Caitlin's long-term goals had changed, but she realized that it would take time before she attained these goals. To make the varsity volleyball team, she would have to continue practicing on the weekends with her friends who were also on the j.v. squad. The varsity had won the state championship last year, and it was considered one of the best teams in the nation. If she made the varsity and played well during her sophomore and junior years, Caitlin believed she would have a good chance at getting a scholarship.

Making the Olympic volleyball squad was another story. This would be a monumental challenge. Caitlin knew that there were thousands of girls who dreamed about making the team, and many were top-notch players. To be selected, she realized that she would have to become a much better player. Caitlin was certain that she could improve her skills at the volleyball camp because the instructors were coaches and players from the best university teams.

To attain her goal of going to a first-rate college, she would need to continue getting good grades. She knew that becoming a marine biologist would require many years of school. She would have to go to college and then to graduate school for a Ph.D. Although Caitlin still wanted to get married some day, have two children, and own a home overlooking the ocean, these were obviously long-term goals!

Caitlin then checked off her short-term goals to see how well she had done during the school year. The study skills program had paid off. She was now carrying an A- in science, and she was carrying B's and B-'s in all her other subjects with the exception of math. Her current grade was C+, but she could still get a B- in the course if she received a B on the final. Caitlin had also attained her short-term goal in volleyball. Her coach said that she was pleased with her progress but that she would have to work even harder next year.

Because she had saved some of her baby-sitting money, Caitlin would soon have enough to pay for half the cost of the volleyball camp. Her parents had agreed to provide the other half of the money as a reward for her hard work

Caitlin was proud of herself. She was already beginning to think about her short-term and long-term goals for next year.

Assessing What You Have Learned about Study Skills

It's time for you to take stock. The following checklist describes the thinking-smart skills you have practiced. Evaluate yourself by putting the appropriate number after each statement.

What I Have Learned Checklist

CODE: 0 = Never 1 = Sometimes 2 = Usually 3 = Always

I can solve problems using DIBS or the 4-Part Problem-Solving System. ____

I establish long-term goals. ____

I establish short-term goals. ____

I set priorities. ____

I develop strategies for getting the job done. ____

I consider the potential consequences before I act. ____

I think about how to avoid predictable problems. ____

I develop a study schedule. ____

I carefully record my assignments. ____

I organize my materials. ____

I study in a quiet, non-distracting environment. ____

I speed-read the unit before reading the material more carefully. ____

I use mind-mapping to understand what I am studying. ____

I take notes from my notebooks. ____

I use highlighters to identify main ideas and details in my notes. ____

I write key facts and concepts on index cards so that I can easily review them. ____

I make powerful associations when I memorize information. ____

I use abbreviations when taking textbook and class notes. ____

I make up practice tests. ____

I prepare for essay tests by answering the title and subtitle questions I have posed. ____

I write down a thumb-nail outline before I answer essay questions on a test. ____

Total Points: ____

If your total is **50 or better,** you can pat yourself on the back! You are studying effectively and thinking strategically. If your score is **below 50,** you need to continue working hard in those areas where you have marked "0" or "1." A **perfect score of 63** indicates that your brain is working so hard, there is probably smoke coming out of your ears!

Reviewing the DIBS Problem-Solving Method

Before you complete the *Winning the Study Game Program*, let's take a few minutes to review **DIBS.** This method can help you handle virtually any problem. As you recall, the acronym **DIBS** stands for:

D(efine) the problem.

I(nvestigate) the causes of the problem.

B(rainstorm) solutions to the problem.

S(elect) an idea to try out.

Situation: You panic when you take a test.

How **DIBS** could be used to solve this problem.

D(efine): I get very frightened when I take a test.

I(nvestigate): I want to do well so badly that I forget what I know.

I am concerned that if I don't do well, it will prove I am dumb.

I spend so much time worrying about the test that I become a nervous wreck.

I expect a disaster to happen, and then it does happen.

B(rainstorm): I could breathe deeply several times, close my eyes, and try to relax while the test is being handed out.

If I begin to panic when I look at the test, I could remind myself that I know the material.

I could visualize (see) myself doing well on the test.

S(elect): I'll use relaxation techniques before the test is handed out.

By thinking strategically, you can analyze the problem, identify the underlying issues, brainstorm a solution, and select the best brainstormed idea to try out and see if it works. If it doesn't, you would then select one of the other brainstorm solutions. If you still can't solve the problems, you could ask your parents or your teacher to brainstorm with you. Sometimes two heads are better than one! The important thing to remember is that most problems can be solved if they are carefully analyzed.

Final Practice with DIBS

Select *one* of the following situations, and use **DIBS** to solve the problem.

Situation: There are too many spelling mistakes on your book reports.

Situation: There are too many careless mistakes on your math homework assignments.

Define: ______________________________

Investigate: ______________________________

____

____

____

Brainstorm: ______________________________

____

____

____

Select: ______________________________

Common Sense and Using Your Head

When you made an error in judgment, your parents may have become exasperated with you and may have said, "Use your head!" or "Show some common sense!" At the time, you may not have really understood what they were saying. You simply knew that they were being critical of you, but you didn't really know what they meant by "show some common sense."

Well, by now you realize that the terms "common sense" and "using your head" mean to *think smart*. This translates into considering your options, weighing the pros and cons, thinking about potential consequences, and figuring out practical solutions to problems.

Let's look at a concrete example of what's involved in *using your head* and *showing common sense.*

Situation: You and a friend are climbing a tree. Your friend tells you to jump from a limb that is about fifteen feet off the ground. You hesitate because you aren't sure if you can jump without hurting yourself. Your friend keeps telling you to jump. You are at the decision point and must decide what to do. What are you thinking about? Ideally, you are thinking about your options. You have four options:

Option #1: You think it's safe to jump, and you jump.

Option #2: You don't think it's safe to jump, and you decide to climb down the tree instead of jumping.

Option #3: You don't think it's safe to jump, but you jump anyway.

Option #4: You don't consider the possible or probable consequences and jump simply because your friend tells you to.

Let's say you choose **Option #1** or **Option #3** and decide to jump. As soon as you hit the ground, you know that you've hurt yourself. When you try to stand up, you can tell that you have injured your ankle. You are barely able to walk, but somehow, with your friend's help, you are able to limp home. Your mom takes you to the emergency room, and the doctor tells you that you have a badly sprained ankle. She tapes it, gives you a crutch, and tells you that you cannot put any weight on your foot for seven days. Because of your injury, you cannot play basketball for the rest of the season.

What would teenagers who have common sense do if they were faced with the same four options? Well, the first thing they would do is consider the potential consequences of each option, and they would quickly rule out **Option #4**. They certainly wouldn't jump simply because a friend told them to. Smart kids think for themselves, and they don't follow others mindlessly.

Smart teenagers would also rule out **Option #3**. If they realize it's not safe to jump and that they are likely to hurt themselves, they would not jump. To do so would be dumb.

Sometimes kids who do have common sense occasionally miscalculate. They may conclude that it's safe to jump **(Option #1)**, and they may sprain their ankle. Despite their normally being smart, they obviously misjudged the speed at which they would descend and the impact when they hit the ground. Having obviously miscalculated, what would they do? If they are in the habit of thinking strategically, they would examine what happened and ask themselves the following questions:

1. **Did I use poor judgment in this situation?**
2. **Did I get hurt simply because of bad luck?**
3. **If I did miscalculate, what could I do to avoid repeating the same mistake next time?**

Teenagers who think smart are determined to learn from their miscues and negative experiences. They may study the wrong material for a test or do something in class that gets them into trouble. Because they are in the habit of using their head, however, they realize they must figure out what went wrong and make the appropriate adjustments.

Teenagers who have common sense try to avoid making mistakes whenever possible. This is especially true in the case of potentially serious mistakes that may involve taking drugs, smoking, drinking, stealing, driving while intoxicated, joining gangs, or painting graffiti on walls and road signs. They say **no** to anyone who suggests they take risks that could potentially produce terrible consequences.

Everyone occasionally makes mistakes and suffers setbacks. The ability to learn from these negative experiences separates kids who use their heads from kids who don't use their heads. If a generally smart kid miscalculates and sprains his ankle jumping off a high tree limb, he would say to himself, "I am certainly not doing that again!" The not-so-smart kid would probably make the same mistake over and over.

What Would You Do?

Situation: You and some friends are on a hike. You discover a cave, and you begin to explore it. Although it's dark inside, you have a flashlight. As you go deeper and deeper into the cave, you discover that there is another passage. You decide to take the path. After about 400 yards, you come to another group of passageways. This time there are four passageways from which to choose. Your friends want to take one, but you are concerned that you may not be able to find your way out. You know that if you get lost, no one would know that you and your friends are in the cave. You are also concerned that if the batteries go dead, you would be in total darkness. You suggest to the others that you return to the entrance. Your friends want to continue exploring.

Your Decision: ______________________________

Your Reasons: ______________________________

____

____

____

Handling Temptations

Training yourself to analyze the pros and cons of situations can be a powerful resource when you are faced with temptations. For example, imagine that you have an important government test on Friday. You plan ahead and schedule time to take notes, identify the important information, memorize key facts, answer title and subtitle questions, make up a practice test, and review your notes and index cards. Your strategy is to do a final review on Thursday night. You want to make sure you that you are as prepared as you can possibly be.

Because you have a church youth group meeting on Thursday night, you decide that you will begin reviewing your notes as soon as you get home from school. On the way home, your best friend suggests you play basketball with some other friends. You really want to play, but you had scheduled the time to study. What should you do? At this decision point, you could use **DIBS** to help you make the right decision.

Define: I want to play basketball with my friend, but I planned to use this time to review for the government test.

Investigate: I worked hard today, and I need to have some fun.

I have already done a lot of studying.

Doing a final review of my notes may not improve my grade on the test.

I promised myself that I would make my very best effort in preparing for the test.

Brainstorm: I could play for a while and then do my studying, assuming there is enough time.

I could keep to my original plan, not play basketball, and study.

I could play basketball tomorrow or over the weekend.

Select: I will keep to my original plan and organize a basketball game after school on Friday or over the weekend.

You will face many temptations in life, and to deal with these temptations appropriately, you must decide what's in your best interest. You could play a game of basketball, or you could improve your chances of getting a good grade on an important test. You have to choose what payoff is most important to you. Dealing with temptations is easier when you have your personal goal clearly in mind and when you logically analyze the situation. If you know what you want and you are using your head, you will usually make the right decision.

Use **DIBS** to deal with the following temptation.

Situation: The football coach thinks that if you lose ten pounds, work out in the weight room, and build your upper-body strength, you can improve your blocking and tackling. You begin to work out and you start to diet, but then you get invited to a birthday party where you know there will be lots of potato chips, soft drinks, ice cream, and cake. You love all these things, and you know it will be difficult for you to resist the temptation. You also know that once you start eating junk food, it's very difficult for you to stop.

Define: ______________________________

Investigate: ______________________________

____

____

____

____

Brainstorm: ______________________________

____

____

____

Select: ______________________________

Deciding What's Smart

Place the following behaviors and attitudes under the correct categories.

tries hard, blames others, complains, bounces back from mistakes and setbacks, procrastinates, shows responsibility, sets priorities, is disorganized, continually interrupts studying, establishes goals, forgets to do assignments, has a messy study area, makes up practice tests, takes notes, writes down assignments, doesn't think about the consequences, doesn't take notes, reviews for tests, studies with the TV on, forgets to take home needed textbooks, identifies important information in notes, does not anticipate what teachers are likely to ask on a test, plans ahead, asks questions when reading, doesn't allow time to proofread reports, hands in sloppy papers, hands in assignments late, budgets time, makes the extra effort to do a first-rate job, creates a quiet study environment, thinks independently, takes excessive risks., keeps track of progress, rewrites messy assignments, develops a personalized study strategy, learns from mistakes

Using Your Head	Not Using Your Head

Feeling Proud, Powerful, and Self-Confident

Few experiences are as thrilling and exciting as achieving an important personal goal. After having completed this program, you deserve to experience this sense of accomplishment. You have worked hard to improve your study and thinking skills and, ideally, you are a much better student than you were several weeks ago. You have every right to feel proud, powerful, and confident.

You now know how to think and study more effectively. The learning process, however, doesn't stop here. To win the study game, you have to use the new skills you've learned *every day*, and you have to apply them whenever you are faced with a challenge, problem, or a barrier in school or outside of school.

You will always carry a powerful tool with you. **This tool is your mind.** You must make a constant habit of using your brain! If you don't, your mind will atrophy like the muscles in your arm when it is in a cast a long time. On the other hand, if you intentionally and regularly use the awesome power of your mind, you'll discover that you can solve virtually any problem you encounter, achieve your personal goals, and learn far more productively. You'll also discover that you are on a track that leads to achievement in all areas of your life.

APPENDIX

Quick Reference Guide

Important Formulas and Methods

DIBS: Problem-Solving Method

D	=	**Define** (the problem or challenge)
I	=	**Investigate** (the causes or symptoms)
B	=	**Brainstorm** (the solutions)
S	=	**Select** (a solution to try out)

4-Part Goal-Setting System (for solving problems)

Step 1 - Define the challenge.

Step 2 - Define a goal that overcomes the challenge.

Step 3 - Establish practical short-term goals.

Step 4 - List specific actions that achieve short-term and long-term goals.

Key Questions When Developing a Strategy

1. What is my goal?
2. What do I already know about this problem or challenge?
3. What steps must I take to get the job done successfully?
4. What possible problems might I face?
5. Who can I ask for help or advice?
6. What research can I do to find out more information?

The "Chewing-Up Information" Method

Step 1 - Turn the main title into a question

Step 2 - Turn each subtitle into a question

Step 3 - Speed-read the material

Step 4 - Re-read the material carefully

Step 5 - Answer the subtitle questions

Step 6 - Answer the title question

MISS RC NAR

Remembering the "Chewing-Up Information" Method

MI	Main-Idea Question
S	Subtitle Questions
S	Speed-Read
RC	Read Carefully
N	Notes
A	Answer Subtitle and Main-Idea Questions
R	Review

Association/Visualization Technique

Step 1 - Write content in color on a card

Step 2 - Tape the card to wall (above eye level to right or left) and visualize with eyes closed

Step 3 - Create a mental picture of content

Step 4 - Write content without looking

General Formula for Study Breaks

6th & 7th Grade - study 20 – 25 minutes before taking a 5 minute break

8th & 9th Grade - study 25 – 30 minutes before taking a 5 minute break

10th & 11th Grade - study 25 – 35 minutes before taking a 5 minute break

Test Relaxation Techniques

Step 1 - Close your eyes and take two deep breaths

Step 2 - Form a positive mental image of succeeding

Step 3 - Silently recite and repeat positive statements

Step 4 - Feel body relax and fear and stress flowing out

ICRA Test Preparation

I **Identify** (important information)

C **Comprehend** (what is being studied)

R **Remember** (key facts)

A **Anticipate** (questions teacher likely to ask)

Comprehensive Test Preparation Strategy

1. Record assignments accurately.
2. Create a quiet and non-distracting study environment.
3. Calculate and budget adequate study time.
4. Speed-read.
5. Mind-map.
6. Ask title and subtitle questions.
7. Read carefully and take notes.
8. Answer title and subtitle questions.
9. Study your notes.
10. Write each main idea on one side of an index card and the details on the other side.
11. Consider what your teacher is likely to regard as important and spend extra time reviewing this information.
12. Make up and answer practice test questions.
13. Do a final test review with a friend and ask each other questions.

Notes:

Notes:

If you have questions, would like to request a catalog, or to place an order, please contact *Peytral Publications, Inc.* We will be happy to help you.

Peytral Publications, Inc.
PO Box 1162
Minnetonka, MN 55345

Toll free order line: (877) 739-8725
Questions: (952) 949-8707
Fax: (952) 906-9777

Or visit us online at:
www.peytral.com